MISSION STORIES FROM HOME AND ABROAD

Faith and Works in Action

Don and Ruth Menkens

MISSION STORIES FROM HOME AND ABROAD

First published 2026

ISBN: 978-1-7644772-2-2 Paperback

ISBN: 978-1-7644772-3-9 E-Book

Contents

DEDICATION

This booklet is dedicated to my dear companion and mother of my children, my Ruth, for her courage and devotion, and also to my five children, Caroline, Wendy, Jennelle, Richard, and Sharon, who endured all sorts of hardships and lack of their "Daddy's" time, while he was off helping the school family.

Thank you for still loving me!

INTRODUCTION TO MISSION SERVICE

As a young boy I grew up in North Queensland. My parents embraced the Seventh-day Adventist faith and each Sabbath, I enjoyed listening to the Mission Stories, of men and women who served God teaching the people about the Gospel, and God's love for them. I determined that I would like to be a missionary one day to go to foreign lands and use my life in service for God. This became my dream and ambition.

After training as a schoolteacher, I married a lovely girl I met at Avondale Missionary College, and after serving as a teacher in state schools in Queensland for some years, I was invited by the church to work as Principal of the Mona Mona Mission school near Kuranda.

Don and Ruth, just married - 19th December 1956

It was a completely new and challenging experience, teaching the aboriginal children, as they were not interested in formal learning. Their main interests lay in Art, Singing and Horse Riding. After just two years, the Mission was closed to make way for a new dam in the area, as we were told. The dam has never been built!

Some of our Mona Mona Senior Girls at Wattle Blossom time.

Jacky Jacky loved to tell stories of former days.

Some of our Mona Mona wild men at Swimming Time.

Mona Mona Mission Station as it was in 1961.

Chapter 1

PAPUA NEW GUINEA

My wife and I and our three girls, Caroline, Wendy and Jennelle were invited to go to work in Papua New Guinea. We were so thrilled with this news, and had visions of a beautiful tropical paradise, with sparkling clear blue seas, golden sandy beaches and coconut trees. Our new school would be at Belepa near the Vailala River in the Papuan Gulf. We flew from Townsville to Port Moresby and then boarded a Catalina Flying Boat which took us to Kerema. As we left Port Moresby and flew west low along the coast, we soon saw dramatic changes as the blue water began to turn to a dirty brown colour, and the beaches turned into black sand. Yes, the coconut trees grew in abundance, but the brown water and black sand beaches came as an unexpected surprise.

Our children enjoyed the flight, and landing on the muddy flood water at Kerema was a really different and somewhat frightening experience, as any small log or floating piece of debris could easily tear open the hull of the plane. A number of Catalinas had already been lost this way and lay buried in the mud at the bottom of the river.

The Catalina landing on the flooded muddy river.

The Landing Barge at Kerema, "ship to shore" with all our luggage.

DIARI 2 at Karo Karo and "Welcome" decorations. Vailala.

After coming to rest, the crew tied the plane to a buoy, and we disembarked onto a small barge with our luggage and were taken ashore.

Then we had to board our small mission launch, the Diari 2, for the four-hour journey by sea to the Vailala River. The trip out to sea and then back into the mouth of the Vailala River was pretty rough, but the worst part was crossing the bar at the river's mouth. The bars are always changing and very rough especially if the tides and outflow from the river conflict with each other, but we made the crossing safely and then sailed up the river to our Mission Headquarters at Karo Karo.

What a sight met us as we tied up at the primitive jetty, which the local people and the Richardson family had bedecked with all sorts of decorations to welcome us. There were lots of palm fronds and all sorts of beautiful flowers, and they were so happy to see us. After a short stay with these dear people, John took us in the big dugout canoe, round the rivers and creeks to our Sawmill.

There we transferred to a trailer hitched to the school tractor, and off we went through the swamp, bumpity bump, over logs placed crosswise on the track through the swamp for about three kilometers to our school at Belepa. What a journey! It was such a relief to finally arrive at our new home on a small hill overlooking the school grounds and the many coconut palms.

A jungle village. Lots of coconuts!

The Belepa "Taxi" from Sawmill to School through the swamps.

The Swamp track. Timber is placed crosswise to stop vehicles bogging.
Not really good for a smooth ride, but necessary.

After settling in and meeting my Headmaster, Apusae, and the rest of my Staff, we began four and a half years of very interesting, sometimes happy and sometimes sad times in service for God with the children and youth in the Vailala area. Belepa was a boarding school, and the students came from lots of different villages scattered across the Gulf and from as far away as Daru in the west at the mouth of the Fly River. There were over two hundred students at the school, and we had six or seven teachers, plus some workers as well, but most of the work depended on the students and teachers.

After Morning Worship in the School Chapel, school classes ran from seven in the morning till 12.30pm. Then it was time for lunch and work assignments all afternoon till 5pm, when we stopped for baths and general home chores and the evening meal. After Evening Worship, the evenings were employed in study period till about 8.30pm and lights out at 9pm.

Food for our students came from our gardens and the jungle. We had sweet potato, taro, taitu yams, breadfruit, pawpaws, citrus, lily-pillies, bananas, peanuts and greens, coconuts, and the staple food of the Gulf coastal people, sago. Because we followed a balanced Work/Study programme, we nearly always had sufficient food for our students and staff.

Work parade was organized every day except Sabbath, and students were assigned in groups with a staff member, to gather coconuts, do dehusking, drying coconuts for copra, weeding gardens was a constant chore, planting gardens, harvesting, building, gathering building material from the bush, making wall matting from the Sago leaf, gathering Biri leaf from the river side to make roof thatching, cleaning dormitories and class rooms, cooks, message and mail crews, and cutting grass around the campus with sarifs which are simply pieces of steel strapping, nearly a metre long, about 25 mm wide and about 2mm thick sharpened on the lower part. The upper end was folded over and wrapped with cloth or a bandage to form a handle. Students took turns in the different work groups to be sure they all had training in every type of activity.

Students dehusking coconuts for Copra.

Teacher's daughter Jennelle helping students process the sago pith.

Nearly every Sunday was Sago-making Day.

Twenty boys and twenty girls with a couple of teachers would select one or two Sago palms somewhere in the surrounding swamps. The palms were then stripped of the large fronds which the girls set up as a factory. The boys would cut the palms down and with a special tool, the pithy starchy inside of the palm was scratched out. The girls would then process this pithy starchy fibre and at the end of the day we would often come home with ten or twelve bundles of Sago starch, each about fifteen to twenty kilos in weight.

See the picture presentation later on in the book for more details of how it is done. Notice how wet Jennelle is. Work must go on rain or shine, and in the Gulf with 360 inches of rain annually, it is mostly rain! There's no shortage of water in the Papuan Gulf!

Our students loved to sing, and we had some great choirs. They seemed to have a natural gift to harmonize, and the resulting music was really delightful. We joined in with other denominational schools sometimes in local eisteddfods and our students outperformed all the other schools at each programme.

I found this part of my mission experience very enjoyable, and especially when our students had completed their studies and requested to be baptized into Christ. We are looking forward to seeing these beautiful young people again in His kingdom, with their teachers and families as well, who were all wonderfully dedicated people, giving their lives in service to the Master.

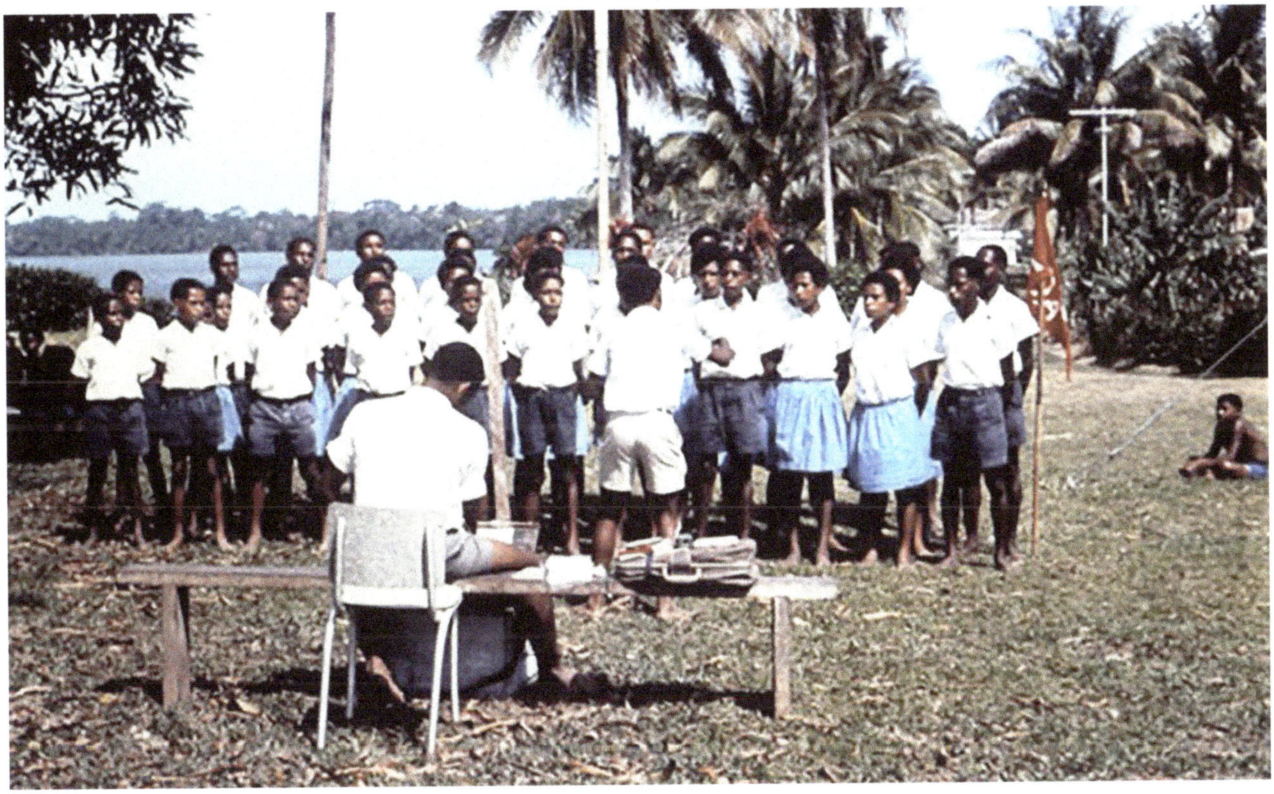

Belepa Primary Choir at Ihu Eisteddfod, took first place.

A large group ready for Baptism at Belepa.

What a joy it was to be able to serve God as a missionary! Maybe some of you might consider training to be a Missionary for God and give your life to help people to know and love our wonderful Saviour and Redeemer. Millions of people in this dark old world still do not know God, and indeed most of this world's people have never even heard the name of Jesus. Can He count on you to be one of His Ambassadors? May the Lord richly bless you as you consider serving Him.

Chapter 2

WHY THE PEOPLE NEED JESUS

We were so shocked at times to see what the primitive heathen people of Papua New Guinea do, that cause untold sickness and suffering and death. Satan surely degrades his people, and it is so good to see these people come out of darkness into the light. Whole villages sometimes accept the Lord and the whole village becomes transformed as a result. It is so wonderful to visit these Christian villages where all is clean, and tidy, in such contrast to the others.

At one village, we had placed a missionary, and I was to visit and take the service one Sabbath. The missionary had built a stout fence around his home and gardens to keep the pigs out. Soon after I arrived, I had a message to use my bowel and asked the missionary where his toilet was. I had to go outside the fence and climb up into a small house on stilts. Inside there was nothing but some coconuts husks, (for toilet paper), and a hole in the floor. I had an urgent message by now, and so had to use the hole, wondering why it was so clean on the ground underneath.

Well, what a shock I was in for! There was a noisy rush underneath and there were two or three big pigs, which cleaned up the droppings very quickly, and then looked up at me as much as to say, "Come on! Haven't you got any more for us?" Yuk!!! I felt like I was going to be sick then and there, but imagine my horror as I rode my little motorbike the thirty miles along the beach on the way home, to see a village woman with the carcass and entrails of a pig spread out along the beach, as she washed it all in the sea water, in preparation for eating it with her family. Nothing of the pig is wasted. It is all eaten. No wonder they have so much disease and sickness.

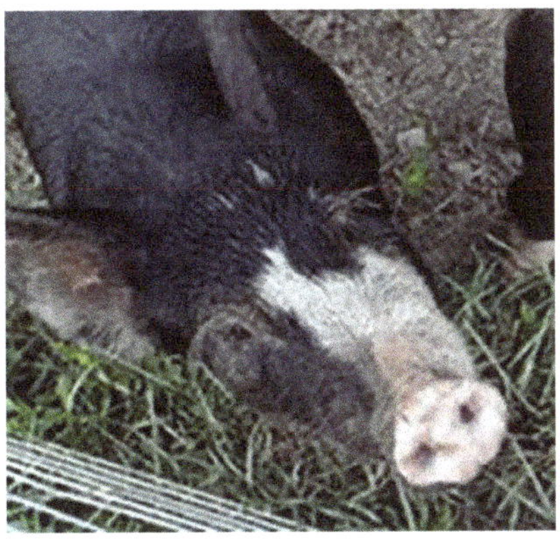

At another village, a government team visited to determine the state of health of the people. They found no less than thirteen people with Leprosy, with one old woman having a very serious contagious kind of Leprosy. She was sitting by the fire handing children some titbits of food and probably handing them some Leprosy as well.

 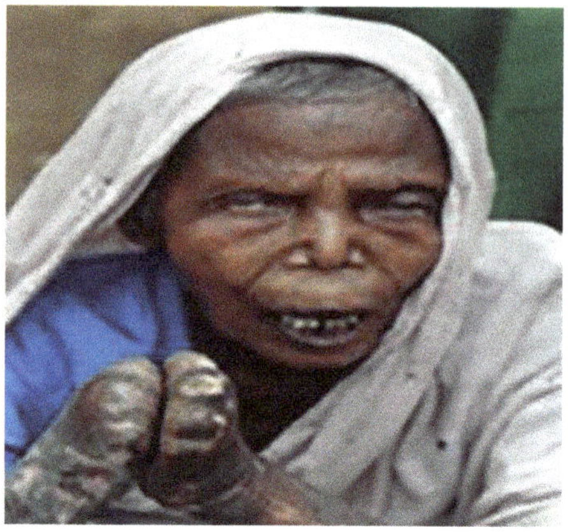

On further investigation it was found that their cemetery was on the side of a hill just upstream from their village. The water they were using from the stream was polluted with juices from the decaying bodies on the hillside and was causing this high incidence of disease. Leprosy is rife in the heathen villages, and it is generally a disease of filth. What a difference it makes when we are able to show them how to clean up their villages and practice good hygiene.

One of the most distressing situations for me happened at Kabiufa. We were about three months into the school year and had a lovely group of students in the high school and college. One strong healthy-looking lad was from an area in the highlands. I have forgotten his name, but not what happened to him. We were so sad to have to send this dear lad home to his village to die. Satan's wages are very nasty indeed.

He gradually became ill, and his features began to distort as though he was laughing. He began behaving in very strange ways and found it difficult to stand and coordinate his movements. Eventually, we had his condition appraised by a doctor as Laughing Sickness, which is peculiar to the area from which he had grown up. Apparently, the villagers in that area practiced a strange ritual. When someone died, they did not bury the person. The body was cooked and eaten by the women and children. The men did not eat of it. The adult men only used the flesh of pigs.

A researcher spent some considerable time in the area and found that the disease was very similar if not the same as Scrapie in sheep, and Bovine Spongioform Encephalitis or Mad Cow Disease. The organism which caused the disease was not a bacteria or virus. It was impossible, he found, to kill the organism with heat, formaldehyde or indeed anything else. It lodged itself in the brain and could take a decade or more to develop into the deadly final symptoms followed by death.

There is no known cure for this disease, Laughing Sickness, and of course we are all familiar with the fact that Mad Cow Disease is also unable to be cured. The outbreak in the United Kingdom some time back, brings home the fact that it may indeed be incubating in people who have eaten of the diseased flesh of so many animals which had the disease and had to be destroyed.

I'M SICK AND TIRED OF BEING FED ANTIBIOTICS, HORMONES, PESTICIDE-CONTAMINATED GRAIN AND GROUND-UP PARTS OF OUR OWN RELATIVES!
Yeah ... me too!
Shut up !!! You're starting to sound like Mad Cows!!!
MAD COWS
JANIK

HMMM!

This is a very strong reason why we have chosen to leave flesh foods right out of our diet. How good it is to be able to teach these people the principles of health and cleanliness to give them hope and a future to look forward to with good health, so they can teach their own people, how to care for themselves, to get well, and stay well. This is the work Jesus commissioned us to do, when He said, "Heal the sick, cleanse the lepers, raise the dead and cast out demons." I look forward to seeing many of these people in God's Kingdom.

Chapter 3

WEDDINGS

Native customs for weddings are interesting occasions. Girls and women are counted as goods and chattels. A father can sell his daughter and demand a "bride-price" from the prospective husband. The price can be a number of pigs, or weapons, or even Bird of Paradise feathers.

Wow! How many beautiful birds were killed for this array?

As we were traveling along the road to Mt Hagen, we came across a display as in the picture above. The "bridegroom" was waiting for the father of the "bride" to arrive to see if he'd accept the bride-price of all these beautiful Bird of Paradise feathers. Imagine how many birds were destroyed to obtain this array.

The women and girls don't have much say over who they marry, and some of the men have a number of wives. The wives do all the work and carry tremendous loads suspended from their foreheads.

Sometimes a woman will have a big bunch of bananas or a baby perched on top as well, while the man walks in front with his machete to "protect" her.

To celebrate the wedding the whole village comes together for a "sing-sing". Usually a number of pigs and chickens are killed and cooked over open fires, and huge quantities of vegetables are prepared in stone ovens or "mumus". To prepare a mumu, a hole is dug in the ground and lined with stones. Then a huge fire is built over the stones until they are very hot, and only the coals are left smouldering. Then the coals are taken out of the hole and the food, wrapped well in banana leaves is laid over the stones, and the coals raked back over the top. A layer of soil is usually placed on top of the coals and the whole thing left overnight to cook. In the morning the oven is opened, and the food is ready to eat. The smell and taste of vegetables cooked like this has to be experienced to be appreciated. All the flavours are sealed in, and the food is delicious!

Our students always had Friday afternoons free to prepare their mumus for Sabbath.

Our Headmaster Anga, and his wife Riva would send up a sample of their Mumu on Sabbath mornings, and we always enjoyed this delicious treat.

Preparing a "Mumu" . Lots of veges wrapped in Banana leaves in an Earth Oven.

One amazing thing we noticed was that the food prepared in this way on Friday, would keep right through the Sabbath hours and still be edible on Sunday, just like the Manna story in the time of Moses. Any food kept overnight on any other day of the week, in the hot, humid tropics, would spoil overnight. Our God still honours those who honour Him and who keep His special Day holy. He is the same wonderful Person Who cared for His children so long ago.

We have had a number of beautiful Christian weddings, during our time in Papua New Guinea and the contrast to the "sing-sings" is quite dramatic. Christian men honour their wives and love them as the Scriptures teach us to do. Here's a picture of Evo and Aita on their wedding day. Evo was a crewman on the Uraheni. Aita is wearing Ruth's veil from when we were married in 1956.

What a clean happy Christian couple they make! In contrast the heathen brides are only partly clothed and smeared with pig grease to make their skin shine. The men are done up with bones in their noses and ears, complete with lots of paint and feathers.

Evo and Aita on their Wedding Day.

Another Chrtistian Wedding at Kabiufa.

This man is typical of village men who dress for special occasions such as "sing-sings," and for heathen weddings.

Here he is parading about soliciting money for taking his picture, at the annual Goroka Show..

What a handsome guy!

This poor widow is mourning the loss of her husband by wearing a head-piece of beads. What a contrast to the Christian ladies!

Chapter 4

LOGGING FOR FEES

The Gulf Mission had established a sawmill near the Headquarters Station at Karo Karo.

The southern highlands people, the Kuka Kukas, consider the upper Vailala River areas belong to them, and so they often cut trees and make rafts which are then floated down to the mission sawmill, and of course they are paid for the logs, giving them a good way to earn some income. The Kuka Kukas are recognized as the fiercest people of Papua New Guinea even though they are very small of stature and considered pygmies. No one dares to upset these people for they do not wait to retaliate fiercely against anyone who is thought to have wronged them, or who poses any sort of threat to them.

At the end of the school year, some of the older students choose to do logging to earn their school fees. With permission from the Mission and an arrangement with the Kuka Kukas, they make a camp far upriver and spend sometimes a few weeks cutting down suitable trees growing near the riverbank, to make a raft. When they have sufficient logs lashed together, they would then guide the log raft downriver to the sawmill, to receive money for their school fees.

On one year end, it was Xmas Day when a group of four students with their tools and supplies climbed into the big mission canoe, ready for me to take them upriver to find a good logging site. We travelled upstream against the current of muddy, turbulent water with lots of floating debris, for about four hours, before deciding on a good spot to make a camp. We unloaded the canoe and set about immediately to make a waterproof shelter for them to live in while they worked. (When they had a raft ready, they would travel downriver to the mill on the raft in two- or three-weeks' time.)

One of the boys went missing for a while, and after an hour or so he returned carrying a harvest of mushrooms he had found. We had not seen this kind of mushroom and so were reluctant to eat any of the ones he cooked up over the campfire. After our meal we all tried to sleep, but it was difficult to find a dry spot under our makeshift shelter. It was my plan to stay overnight and then return home to Belepa in the morning.

It was about seven o'clock when we were all awakened abruptly by the cries of pain from the lad who had eaten the mushrooms. Only the glow of the dying campfire gave any light, to dispel the pitch blackness of the jungle night but we quickly located a torch and found our student writhing in pain holding his stomach, and of course, we knew instinctively that he had indeed eaten some poisonous kind of mushrooms, and there was only one thing to do.

As quickly as possible we put him into the canoe, with his gear and mine and set off downriver in the pitch darkness with only a torch, for the Government Aid Post at Ihu. Going downriver was much easier and faster, as we now had the current with us, but we still had to hope and pray that we did not hit any logs or debris that could capsize our canoe and throw us into the murky, brown, crocodile-infested water.

After about two hours we saw the lights of the Ihu Station, and we were so thankful to have had an uneventful trip. As we neared the jetty, a most amazing sight met our eyes. There was a huge tree near the jetty, and it was wonderfully lit up with myriads of flashing lights. My first thought was that they had decorated the tree somehow with Xmas lights. It was truly an amazing sight. When we drew closer however, we found it was a flowering tree and was absolutely covered with fireflies, all flashing their tiny lamps.

The Medical Orderly was eventually found, and he immediately inserted a tube down into the lad's stomach and pumped the poisonous contents out with a special pump. The student recovered quickly and next morning was fine.

I will never forget that frightening trip down the wild river in pitch darkness, nor the amazing sight of all those fireflies. They reminded me of God's promise in Psalm 34. The angels of the Lord are there to protect the Lord's people, and we were so grateful to Him for protecting and caring for us on that fearful canoe trip with a very sick boy. He is indeed a wonderful Lord!

Colin Winch explaining the wonders of flight to some Kuka Kuka warriors.

Peruka, Vai, and mill hand working at our Vailala Mill.

Motoring down the Vailala in the big canoe, to Ihu Government Station.

Chapter 5

MUSIC

That the Lord loves good music, is obvious as we listen to the sounds of nature around us every day. If you are fortunate enough to live in a rural area, you will be able to appreciate the songs of the birds, and all the calls of different wildlife of land and sea.

The angels sing to praise their Creator and to extol His love for all His creation. Even the stars have their own distinctive sounds scientists tell us today. What a joy the Creator must have had as He organized all the different sounds!

The boys and girls of our Mission schools loved to sing and our daily morning and evening worship times, and especially on Sabbaths, were a real joy to me. The students seemed to have a natural ability to harmonize, and it is a real treat to hear them sing. My own love of good music inspired me to train our young people into choirs and we invariably would take first place in local eisteddfods, in the Gulf and also at Kabiufa in the highlands.

While at Kitomave School near Kikori, the London Missionary Society folks at Baimuru invited us to participate in their Music Festival. A number of schools would be attending, and we agreed to be there as well. It was about a two-hour journey for us by canoe and outboard through the maze of delta rivers and creeks, so when the time came, we loaded our school choir of about twenty-five students into our big canoe and set off early in the morning. It was low tide, and we were travelling carefully along when on the sloping bank above us, as huge crocodile went scurrying down the bank and slid into the water ahead of us.

Looking back on that trip now, I wonder how we would have fared if the motor had broken down or we had some other mishap. We had no communications, and it was not a very hospitable place especially with lots of nasty mosquitoes and ugly crocodiles lurking in the water or sleeping on the mud banks. We saw a number of these creatures at close quarters as we travelled but we were able to arrive safely, and had a wonderful time of fellowship, praise and sharing with students and teachers from other schools. Fortunately, all went well on the return trip with the tide in and flowing with us, and we arrived home safely before nightfall.

At Kabiufa, four of our boys formed a quartet and sang a number of the King's Heralds Songs for us. They did extremely well at imitating these professional singers from America who visited Kabiufa with H.M.S. Richards Jnr while we were there.

Chapter 6

KATA RAGOSO

I was just a young boy of nine or ten years of age, and each Sabbath day, my parents and I, and young brother Terry, would attend worship services held in a hall on Stanley Street in Townsville. I particularly remember one Sabbath, when we had some special visitors from the Islands. They had come down to Australia to pick up a new Mission ship for the Solomon Islands. There was a white Pastor with some island people, and they were stopping over in Townsville for the Sabbath before going on to the Solomon Islands as I remember.

One of the crew members was a tall Solomon Islander. His skin was as black as pitch, and when he spoke or smiled his pearly white teeth made such a contrast, as did the whites of his eyes set in his coal black face, under a large mop of black fuzzy wuzzy hair. He didn't wear trousers either but had a sort of heavy black skirt wrapping round him and held with a belt. It was called a Lap Lap, and he also wore a lovely white shirt and tie, and sandals on his feet.

His name was Kata Ragoso and is pronounced with the "ng" sound as "Rangaso". I had never seen anyone like this before and was absolutely awed by his stature and bearing. Imagine my interest and surprise when he was asked to tell a mission story for the Sabbath School. He began by thanking everyone for welcoming them to Townsville and then proceeded to tell the following story.

During the war, the Japanese had taken over the Solomon Islands and had commandeered many of the local villagers as their porters and workers. Kata Ragoso was among the ones working for the Japanese, with one of his friends. They worked faithfully all week, but when it came to Friday afternoon, Kata went to the officer in charge and told him they would not be working the next day, Saturday, as it was the Sabbath.

The Japanese Officer became very angry and told Kata in no uncertain terms that he would work and do as commanded or suffer severe punishment. Kata tried to explain, but the officer only became more and more angry and even hit Kata around the head with the butt of his revolver several times.

When Kata still refused to work on the Sabbath, the officer ordered him and his friend to be put into prison ready to be shot in the morning! Accordingly, they were tied up and marched off to the prison enclosure. The room was locked tightly and had a guard at the door and the surrounding fence which had a gate, was padlocked and guarded by two sentries as well. There seemed no way out, and it appeared to be certain death in the morning, for the both of them.

All the faithful villagers were earnestly praying for them, and they were trusting in the Lord to care for their faithful brethren. Kata and his friend tried to sleep but were awakened during the night by a person who said,

"Get up and come with me." They stood up and noticed that the ropes tying them had been removed. The door of the room opened, and the visitor walked out past the guard and beckoned them to follow. They came to the outer gate, which opened of its own accord for them, and the guards did not seem to know that they were passing through the gate in front of them. As soon as they were through, the gate closed behind them as had the door of the room.

The visitor lead them down the path to the bay, and there on the beach was a canoe with two paddles. The visitor told them to get into the canoe and go to their village. When they turned to thank the visitor, there was no one there. Now they know for sure that God had sent His angel and had freed them and saved them from certain death. Kata and his friend were able to keep well clear of these Japanese people until the war ended soon afterwards. It reminded us all of the experience of Peter and the apostles who were also rescued from prison by angels, as told in the Book of Acts.

Kata told us this story himself, and I was spellbound by it. Right then and there I wanted to be a Missionary and determined in my heart that one day I would work for God as His emissary in the island fields. I so much wanted to help the many heathen people in the island fields to know Jesus and His saving grace, like Kata Ragoso. It was a great privilege later on in life to be invited to work as a Missionary Teacher in Papua New Guinea for eleven years. It was so wonderful to be part of God's plan, and to see so many young people and older ones accepting Jesus as their Saviour and giving themselves to Him and His service.

Chapter 7

RICHARD'S EXIT AND ENTRY

We were stationed at Belepa and Ruth was about six months on the way with our son Richard. She woke me one Sabbath morning and said she was haemorrhaging lightly. When we live in such an isolated area, with no telephone, or radio communications, we must rely on the Lord completely, so we gathered our staff and some strong student boys to help. After special prayer, we made a crude stretcher using some bags and poles, and with Ruth aboard, we hoisted her to the shoulders of four strong students, and set out with our three children in tow, to take her to the mission head-quarters at Karo Karo, about five miles away.

Their radio was not working, so I hitched a ride with a passing K-Boat on its way to Ihu Government Post, while Ruth rested at the home of the Richardsons at Karo Karo. John, the Mission President, was away at the time on the Mission ship the Uraheni. There was no one medically able at Ihu, so I borrowed their Land Rover and drove as quickly as possible to Orokolo, about twenty miles west, where there was an LMS Clinic and a trained sister. She graciously agreed to come back with me, and she also offered to accompany us to Kerema, if we could catch the outgoing K-Boat which was heading back to Moresby. They would stop at Kerema where there was a resident Government Doctor stationed. It was about three hours by sea to Kerema, and the trip was uneventful. Ruth lay quietly in a bunk with the sister close by and did not even get sea-sick. The children enjoyed all this drama and the boat ride.

Orokolo had radioed Kerema and they knew we were coming. In fact, the District Officer's wife prepared a vacant house for us, and even provided a big basket of food and goodies for us, which was so good of her.

The doctor was an old German fellow, and after he examined Ruth, he prescribed complete bed rest, and gave us some powerful sleeping pills, which I promptly put out of harm's way up in the ceiling. We had to wait for a few days till Wednesday when the Catalina Flying Boat was due, and Ruth was taken to Port Moresby.

Catalina Landing at Kerema

The Lemke's met her and installed her with our three children in the Mission Hostel. The LMS sister and I returned to our posts, to carry on with our respective responsibilities.

The August school holidays arrived, and Ruth and the three girls went up to Bisiatabu to stay with some lovely folks there. On the last Sabbath afternoon of August, Ruth lost quite a large clot of blood, and these kind folks took her through to the Hospital at Moresby. The Oemke's who were at Bautama School took Caroline and Wendy, so they could continue their school lessons with Mrs Oemke, while Jennelle stayed with the Bisiatabu folks.

Ruth spent all of September, in the Hospital, and on yet another Sabbath morning, early on the 21st of September, Ruth started contractions, which continued right through till about one o'clock every three minutes. It was a slight Placenta Privea that caused all this drama, and when Richard was still not making his appearance, the lady doctor decided to do a Caesarian Section at 2pm. When Ruth came to at about 4pm, Mrs Oemke was there and told her she had a son. Ruth said, "Oh, Don will be happy!" and she promptly fell asleep again. Don did not find out till Monday when he radioed through to Moresby Hospital from Mission Headquarters at Karo Karo and spoke to Ruth personally to see what was happening. It was very difficult for us all working in such an isolated place, but we found some very kind caring people, and thank God for them, and their help, in time of need.

Don with Son Richard

Chapter 8

MISSIONARIES NEED TO BE INNOVATIVE

THE PEANUT PLANTER

We needed to plant peanuts. Our tractor had readied the area, but how were we going to plant in straight rows evenly spaced, so that we could cultivate the patch with the tractor to save work and time. Hmmm! We would make a many-legged peanut planter!

A long piece of bamboo was cut, and we marked the bamboo at even intervals with a machete. We placed the bamboo parallel with the edge of the field and had twenty students stand behind the bamboo at each mark. Each student was given a small quantity of peanuts, and instructed on how to plant each nut, exactly behind the mark on the bamboo pole. A string line was stretched along one side, and the bamboo was moved up the string line as the planting proceeded. "One step—plant seeds—One step--plant seeds—One step –plant seeds", and on and on up the field keeping the end of the bamboo right on the string line.

This arrangement worked really well, and we soon had the field all planted with the rows all spaced equally and all in line. I'm not sure how many peanuts were planted in their mouths, but we always had lots of volunteers for this activity.

It was very hot when we did the planting and it was very interesting to watch some of the students cut some palm fronds and in a matter of minutes, they could weave themselves a very effective and shady hat.

As the plants grew, we were able to cultivate the rows easily and quickly with our tractor and cultivating implement. When the peanuts were fully grown and ready to harvest, the students learnt how to pull the peanuts and stook them to dry in the sun when we had some sunshine.

They loved peanuts and it was good for them too, providing extra protein in their mainly starchy diet.

OUR SPRING WATER

We had a lovely spring, which we used for drinking water and for washing, but we had a major problem. The hole was always getting covered with debris from the surrounding jungle trees and vines. Also, the water was often being fouled by people, and by dipping their sometimes dirty containers directly into the water.

So, I devised a plan to enlarge the hole and build a concrete wall across the lower end with a fifty-millimeter galvanized steel pipe cemented into the wall pointing upwards to the outlet, so that the inlet of the pipe would always be under water. This would get rid of the blocking problem from leaves and other debris.

When the teachers saw that I was placing the pipe in the wall sloping upwards to the outlet, they laughed at me, and even the headmaster assured me that water would not run up the pipe. Well, I told them to be patient and watch what happened when the water level rose to near the top of the wall. I had purposely set the outlet end of the pipe about a hand width below the level of the top of the wall.

They watched incredulously as the water rose higher and higher and eventually flowed out of the outlet end of the pipe with a full flow! The inlet end of the pipe was about four inches below the surface of the water, which prevented leaves and other debris from blocking the inflow. That beautiful spring water served us well for years, never blocking up, and never again did anyone have to foul the upstream water. There was enough room even below the outlet for our students to wash clothes and even to shower themselves.

DOCTOR DON

It was work time again, and a number of our students were clearing more jungle to make areas to plant our sweet potato and taro at our new school at Kitomave. They usually used axes and machetes for this work. With the constant rain nearly all year round, everything is wet constantly and sometimes becomes very slippery to work cutting the bush back.

One of our boys did slip one afternoon, and somehow managed to slide his hand down the sharp side of his machete. It cut deeply into the palm of his hand but fortunately did not sever any of the tendons.

When some of his workmates brought him to me, I was shocked as it was a really nasty gash about seventy-five millimeters long and gaping open whenever he opened his hand. It was obvious that the wound would need stitching together if it was to heal properly and not cripple the use of his hand.

We had left our school medical attendant at Belepa, to care for the Dispensary there for the lower school and the local villagers, so guess who had to do the sewing up? I asked my wife for one of her needles and some cotton, and my small pliers. We did not have any anaesthetic, so we used some ice from the fridge to numb the hand somewhat and I proceeded to use the pliers and needle and thread to draw the sides of the wound together.

The student was very brave, and eventually we had about seven or eight stitches in and tied with a surgeon's knot that I had learnt to tie in Pathfinders. We then poured copious amounts of Acriflavine over the now-closed wound and bandaged it all up neatly. It healed over nicely, and when a doctor visited Kikori about two weeks later, I took the student to him to check on the healing process.

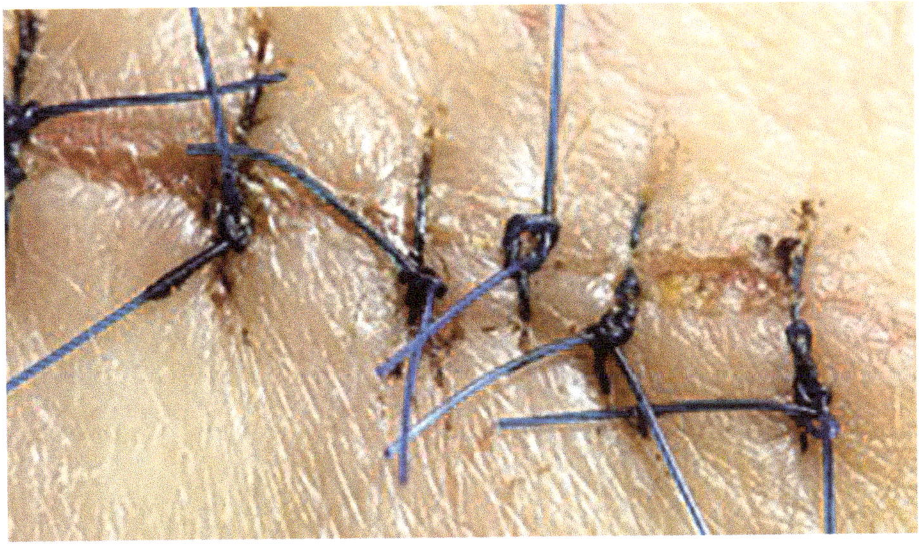

After examining the hand, he said, "Well, that's a neat suturing job, if ever I saw one!" I was so thankful that there was no infection and the boy's hand was soon as good as new.

So, missionaries really need wisdom and innovative abilities if they are to be successful workers for God. I am reminded of the counsel from God's Word found in James 1, that if we ever need wisdom, we need to ask God in faith for it, and He will provide the ideas, and skill we need to accomplish any task He sets us. His biddings are His enablings!

Chapter 9

WE ARE OPEN BIBLES KNOWN AND READ OF ALL MEN

Maira coconut plantation on the Vailala River was about five miles from our school at Belepa. We would sometimes go down to visit the plantation owner to send radio messages or take copra to be sent off to market. The road was very primitive, and the bridges over streams were very old and shaky, especially for the heavy tractor and trailer.

One day when we made the trip, with a number of students on board, it was raining fairly heavily as usual, but we made it safely to the plantation, and the manager came out to greet us. Where we pulled up there were lots of very muddy dirty holes where the pigs were want to wallow in the slops. As I stepped down off the tractor, somehow, I lost my balance, slipped and fell down into one of these nasty smelly holes. It was not a wonderful experience to be sure, but I just tried to brush off the muddy mess and never said a word.

The manager just stood there with an astonished look on his face. It must have been only seconds, but it seemed like a long time before he said anything. When he did speak, he said,

"Well, I have never in my life seen anyone have such a nasty experience and not say a bad word! That's amazing!"

He was a big man and quite a kind fellow really. He took me into the house and let me shower and clean up. Then he handed me a set of his clean clothes to put on. I looked really funny in these oversized shorts and shirt, but I was truly grateful to him for his kindness, and it was so good to feel clean again.

We had a great visit, with his wife and daughter as well, and I was able to share God's love and His goodness with them, which of course would not have happened had I started swearing and cursing about my misfortune. We surely are open books, and others read us every day by our actions and especially our words, for our words are but a reflection of our thoughts. Let us guard our thoughts and words carefully, so others will see that Jesus lives in us. Look at Ephesians 3:2 and Romans 8:28.

I couldn't help thinking of the old adage, "I'd rather see a sermon than hear one any day!" and I was so glad I had controlled my words and feelings.

On the way home from that trip, as we were crossing one of the bridges, the main log under the right-hand side broke and we slid down into the creek. Fortunately, it was not very deep. No one was hurt but there was nothing we could do to rescue the tractor and trailer. So, we just had to leave it there overnight, and the next day we brought the school children and staff to help. We tied lawyer vines and ropes to the tractor after removing the trailer pin, and then with everyone pulling in unison, and lots of praying, and shouting, we were able to move the tractor out of the creek and on to level ground. We then pulled the trailer out and re-hitched it to the tractor. What a happy band we were as we made our way back to the school with our precious tractor.

This also taught us a great lesson. We might not have much strength on our own, but when we all pull together as one with the Lord on our side, we can accomplish what sometimes may seem impossible tasks. See Romans 8:31.

Chapter 10

DID YOU REALLY UNDERSTAND?

In class one day with my Year Sevens, I asked them to do a task, and one older lad, (I believe his name was Koivi), responded in Motu, "Lau komenai diba lasi!" "Komenai", I understood, meant "to hear", and I believed he was saying, "he could not hear me!" So I spoke louder, but he responded in the same way, "Lau komenai diba lasi!" I thought that was very strange, so spoke even louder, but had the same response, "Lau komenai diba lasi!" By now the whole class was looking very amused, so I asked them why they were all smiling.

Apparently, in Motu, "komenai" also means "to obey", and what he was really saying was that he did not want to do the task I was asking him to do. Eventually I got to the bottom of the problem, and all was well again, but it taught me a great lesson.

How often we respond to God in a similar way. We hear what He says to do but often we want to do our own way instead, and do not want to trust and obey His commands or His leading in our lives. We need to take God at His Word and trust Him explicitly.

"Trust and obey for there is no other way,

To be happy in Jesus, but to Trust and Obey."

On another day, it was mid-afternoon, and the student body was about the daily work programme, when a boy came running up to me, calling out in Pidgin English, "Jimmy im fall out long coconut tree and i dai!" This was startling news to me, as we certainly were always careful to avoid accidents, and telling the parents that their child had died at school was a very serious matter, sometimes with nasty reprisals.

So I ran quickly back with the boy, and to my amazement found Jimmy sitting up and alive. He had indeed fallen down from the palm tree, had winded himself and was temporarily unconscious.

When I chastised the messenger for saying that Jimmy died, a teacher came to his rescue and explained that in Pidgin English, "Jimmy dai" means he is unconscious. If the person was really dead, they would say, "Jimmy dai finis." I was so glad that Jimmy did not "dai finis." That was another lesson for the new expatriot teacher from Australia. It is not good to make a judgment if one does not fully understand what is being said and meant.

English is a very expressive language, and the same thing can be said in many different ways, but in Motu, the language of Papua, or in Pidgin English, if something is good , "Ia be namo!" or "Im gutpela." If it is very good, "Ia be namo herea!" or "Im gutpela tru." There are no more ways to describe the goodness of something. This was very humourously depicted when we had a visiting speaker, Pr Lyn Uttley, from South Australia, visit our school. He took a meeting for the whole school one evening and Ehopea, one of our teachers, was interpreting into Motu for the village folks. Pr Uttley was describing the beauties and joys of heaven. It was a beautiful place, and Ehopea translated, "Ia be namo." Pr Uttley went on to say it was wonderful, glorious, marvelous and on and on. Each time Ehopea would translate, "Ia be namo herea!" "Ia be namo herea!" "Ia be namo herea!"

Eventually Pr Uttley stopped and looked directly at Ehopea with a questioning look, which clearly said, "You are not translating what I say to the people." When it was explained to him, he also learned the lesson I had earlier learned. We really need to know all the facts before we make a judgment.

Chapter 11

GAMAI

One of my students came from a former cannibal village in the western Gulf. His people had actually cooked and eaten a couple of white missionaries, not long before he came to school, but somehow the Gospel had gained access to their village, through one of their own people who had accepted Jesus elsewhere, and he was able to convince the whole village of God's love for them. That's how Gamai came to be able to attend school with us, and he was our engine boy. It was his job to care for the diesel engine driving the generator for our lights in the evenings for study time etc. I tried repeatedly to get Gamai to let me know when the diesel was low so that I could order some more from Moresby, but inevitably Gamai would forget and only let me know when the diesel was all gone, leaving us without lights for a week or so.

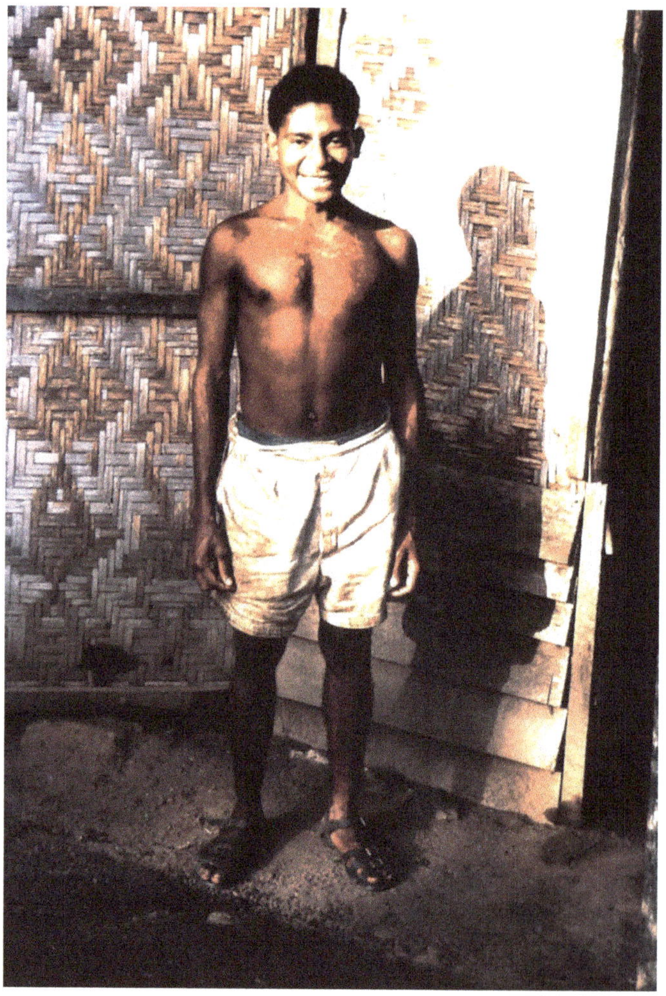

Gamai's village was built on tall poles implanted in the mud at low tide. When the tide came in, the water acted as a sea-food supply, as well as a sewer, and also as a barrier against other tribes raiding their village. When the tide was out, the mud was also a barrier to attackers. Because of the filth and lack of hygiene, there were numerous cases of leprosy among these people.

They lived very primitively on sago and fish and a few other items from their gardens, and their transport was in special dugout canoes, which were simply hollowed out logs open at each end and slightly bent down in the middle. Because of the heavy rainfall in the Gulf, the canoes fill with water. Being open each end allows the people to swish the canoe back and forth, to the left and then to the right, which causes the water in the canoe to fly out each end, and quickly empty ready for use. The paddler stands in the middle of the canoe and can paddle for hours standing. I tried standing and paddling but lost my balance and ended up in the water every time!

One of the practices of Gamai's people was ear lobing. They would pierce the ear lobe and then insert a piece of stick to keep the hole open. After it healed, they would insert another stick a little larger and so on till the ear lobe was quite huge. Gamai arrived at school, about sixteen or seventeen years old, with these huge ear lobe rings, and soon became the laughingstock of the school children, which upset him somewhat.

When checking the roll one morning I noticed Gamai was not in class and sent one of the lads to see if they could find him. The boy came back very frightened saying that Gamai was in the dormitory and had blood all over him, we rushed over to see what was wrong and found he had taken a razor blade and had cut off the offending rings from his ears. Hence the extensive bleeding. Well, we cleaned him up and patched him up as best we could. He healed up well, and the students did not tease him anymore.

When Gamai finished his schooling with us he went to Bible Training School and became a missionary to his people. God can use anyone who will offer their lives in service to Him, even people who have been cannibals!

Chapter 12

PLAYING CRICKET AT SEA

On a beautiful morning, the Mission Ship, the URAHENI, was sailing west across the Papuan Gulf to enter the mouth of the mighty Turama River, for a Camp Meeting some miles upstream. The ship was loaded with delegates, speakers and other passengers, and we were all enjoying the voyage.

We were well out in the Gulf when, without warning, the ship hit a submerged sandbank. She rose up and just sat still with the big eight-cylinder Gardner diesel still turning the propeller, but we weren't going anywhere!

The sudden violent jolt threw us all forward, but no one was seriously hurt. Captain William, and as many as were able, jumped overboard and tried to push the ship back into deeper water, but it was all in vain. The current was far too swift, and in a matter of minutes, there was a huge hole on the upstream side of the ship, and a corresponding mountain of sand on the downstream side.

We were apparently off the mouth of one of the huge Gulf Rivers, and with the tide running out as well, this caused the huge sandbank to form way out at sea. These sandbanks apparently are always shifting and so are not able to be permanently marked on maps.

Plenty of time to do all sorts of "catch up" work, and play!

Ehopea, one of the teachers, (RHS) and a student lad inspecting the backend.

It was very obvious that we weren't going anywhere for quite a while, till the tide returned. Within ten to fifteen minutes, we were high and dry, and could disembark to explore the massive sand-bank, and inspect the bottom of the ship. We had at least eight to ten hours to "kill", so some went walking, some caught up on some sleep, stretched out on the sand, others did some personal grooming cutting each other's hair, while the rest of us formed teams and played cricket right next to the ship out at sea!

Eventually, about ten hours later, we were afloat again, and able to continue on our way to the Camp Meeting, a little late, but very thankful that neither the ship nor any of us were seriously hurt.

The Turama River is usually very dirty brown water due to the heavy rains that almost continually fall in the Gulf area. Where we had the Camp Meeting, was at a small village up one of the small tributaries of the Turama, and it was perfectly clean clear water. We were able to see right to the bottom, and all the bottom of the ships as well. We tied up next to the DIARI, the mission launch from Daru.

It was spectacular to see the two ships side by side in this absolutely clear water. The water flowing from this beautiful clear stream, pushes out into the muddy Turama water, for some distance before it takes on the colour of the river water.

I couldn't help thinking how Christians sometimes move out into the world and soon they look like the world as well. Only the washing of the blood of Jesus can keep us "unspotted by the world".

We had quite a number of experiences to share with the Campers, and had a wonderful time studying the Word, and sharing the blessings of the Lord, with these dear people.

Sister ships—URAHENI and DIARI 2—in a crystal clear stream off the Turama.

Chapter 13

THE NEW SCHOOL AT KIKORI

Our school at Kitomave, on the Kikori River in the Papuan Gulf, was a new school we were establishing for our upper primary students. We were given $300 and 300 acres of virgin jungle to start with.

Kitomave from the mission aircraft January 1968

Kitomave from the mission aircraft May 1968—now self-sufficient for food.

Our school at Belepa, was infested with Nutgrass, and we had very limited land to grow enough food for over two hundred students plus staff. We took two of our teachers and myself, and Years 4-7, about fifty students, to start with. We knew it was going to be a real challenge to clear the jungle and get gardens established, as soon as possible. The mission ship was loaded with all the necessary desks and furniture, and the tractor and trailer, on different trips to transport everything needed to the new school.

Loading Uraheni at Moura Plantation, with supplies for the new school.

Negotiating the small delta waterways. Pr Lester Locke on board.

Because of the heavy rainfall, the huge rivers were always in flood, and the deltas were just a maze of creeks and waterways. It was possible to sail about one hundred kilometers from east to west without going out to sea, just by using the deltas. Of course, it is also very easy to get lost in such a maze, and we were so glad to have Captain William to negotiate a safe passage through to the new location.

Jungle giants with huge fluted roots making way for school gardens.

Sheltering from the rain under a fluted root.

The jungle at Kitomave had many huge trees, some with fluted roots, and we only had axes and hand tools to work with. So, Pr John Richardson, President of the Gulf area, bought us a small chainsaw. I distinctly remember the afternoon he delivered it and showed me how to use it. We were so excited to have this modern tool to help with clearing, but it was now late in the afternoon, so trying it out would have to wait till the morning.

Clearing some spaces to plant our food crops. Too wet to burn, so everything has to be chopped and put in heaps to eventually rot down.

Headmaster Anga felling a jungle giant.

Taro Kong Kong planted in the cleared spaces.

Taro, Corn, Kau Kau (Sweet Potato) thriving in the rich soil.

We had just finished building a new chook yard and hen house, near our home, and early in the morning, I was up bright and early to try out the new chainsaw on a big tree just outside the corner of the chook yard. I felt confident I knew how to cut down a tree, so checked which way I wanted it to fall, away from the chook house and yard, and began making a notch in one side. I then made a cut on the other side and expected the tree to fall away from the yard and chook house.

Well, the tree had ideas of its own it seems, for it fell down right on the middle of our new chook house, and in my rush to use the saw, I hadn't let the chooks out! Oh dear, what a mess! When we eventually cut the tree up and carted it away, we found a couple of paper-thin chooks under the tree, and of course, we had to start all over again with building another house for the survivors!

It was a real challenge for us all at Kitomave. Ruth had to teach our four children, Caroline, Wendy, Jennelle, and Richard. This was a great challenge for her, especially with baby Sharon vying for her attention. To ease the burden, I took Caroline with me to the school building, and she worked there on her correspondence lessons under my supervision while I taught the indigenous students. The nearest ex-patriot woman to our school was about three kilometers downriver, and in hindsight, it would have been great if Ruth and the children could have visited with Dot Richardson, or later, Dulcie Parker at the Headquarters Station. The only transport was via the river, and it was really difficult to work this into the school programme. I would find it difficult to leave the school for an afternoon, and I would not be comfortable allowing my family to travel on the river without me.

Gulf Mission Headquarters about three kilometres downstream from Kitomave.

Principal's home under construction.

Our home was almost complete, when we arrived. A builder from Australia had put up the house, plus two teachers' homes, and some of the school building.

The girl students used the second teacher's house as a dormitory. The married teacher, Anga. from the Solomons, and his wife Riva and two children, had the other teacher's home. Anga was an excellent headmaster, and very capable with his hands as well. I taught him to use the chainsaw, and he did a fine job with it, in the school gardens, well away from our chook house! He could turn his hand to many things including assembling water tanks.

Anga and a student assembling a water tank for the school.

It was impossible to burn anything because of the constant rain, so we had to just cut everything up and pile it into heaps, making clearings to plant our sweet potato, and taro, and other veggies. School classes were Monday to Friday from 7am to 12 noon. Then we had lunch, and everyone worked in the gardens all afternoon rain or shine, but mostly rain! However, in three months we had enough food to feed the student body and the teachers, but this was heavily reliant on the local Sago Palms, which grew everywhere in the swamps.

The leaves are used as funnels and to hold the pith while the girls hit it to loosen the starch.

A typical set up for processing the Sago Pith.

Every Sunday was Sago making day. Twenty boys and twenty girls would pair off, and head for the swamps with one of the teachers. One or two Sago palms would be cut down, by the boys. The huge leaves were used as funnels set up by the girls on forked sticks, and another soft wide part of a palm tree was formed into a basket to act as a receptacle for the water and starch to run into at the thin end of the funnel.

Our eldest girl Caroline helping the students. Note how wet she is from the constant rain.

Little sister Jennelle loved to help too.

The boys would bark the palm in about metre sections, and with a special tool, (a short piece of sharpened thirty-millimeter pipe on a forked stick), would chip out the pithy middle of the palm and take the pith to the girls, who put it into the wide top of their leaf funnels.

Student boys removing the inner pith for the girls to process.

The inner top of the palm makes great eating also. Tastes like almond nut.

Koivi entertaining to keep everyone happy.

They would then hit it with a stick to break it up finely, releasing lots of the starch, which ran down with copious amounts of water through a sieve, into the receptacle on the ground. At the end of the day, the receptacle could hold up to 50 kgs of Sago starch, which the boys would press into specially woven packs which were then tied to poles and carried home by two boys on each pole, to the school storehouse.

Taking home the results of the day's work. Food supply for one week.

During the week the students assigned as cooks, would stuff some of this sago into special thin bamboo sections and cook it over an open fire. When cooked, the bamboo was peeled away to reveal a long jelly-like end-product, about 450mm long. It was quite nutritious and looked quite comical as the students wound it round their arms as they munched away from end to end.

Our single teacher initially lived in with the boys in a makeshift long hut of corrugated iron, beside the river, until the girls' dormitory was completed, and his teacher's house was free for him to use. There were some very stressful times as you can imagine but usually everyone pulled their weight and were happy to have this new location for our school.

Pr John Richardson was a very practical man. He had seen some limestone cliffs up river a little way from the school, which he thought would be an ideal resource for making concrete blocks for our buildings. He somehow located a small Rock Crusher in Sydney and had it sent up to our school. He bought a Lister two-cylinder diesel engine to drive it and we set it up near the river.

Preparing the Limestone for the Crusher.

He made up some special tools to make holes into the limestone, out of twenty-five-millimeter galvanized water pipe. One end was cut like a "V", and then he taught us how to keep hammering the tool directly into the limestone, turning the pipe at each hit. This made a hole about six hundred millimeters deep, in an hour or so of hitting and turning.

The next process the students loved to watch at a safe distance. I would load the holes with gelignite primed with a cap and fuse. I would light the fuses and run for cover, while the explosions took place. When it was all quiet again, we would load the rocks into our big dugout canoe, and head for home downriver, sometimes with only inches of freeboard. I made up a winch and derrick on the riverbank, and the students would haul the rocks up out of the canoe and pile them up ready for the crusher. We had two bins, for coarse, which went on to the roads, and medium/fine which we used to form our concrete blocks. Because of the limestone, the blocks looked really a beautiful white when dry and were very strong. We used these blocks to build the girls' dormitory and the school, and the boys' dormitory.

It was very interesting to see these young students working the Rock Crusher, and the sieves over the bins, and making the blocks, but they worked very well, and seldom complained, as they saw the results of their labours.

Crushing the limestone for our next stage—brick-making.

The Brick-making Team, with the boys on Cook Duty in the background.

Concrete Blocks made from the Limestone ready for the new Girls' Dorm. Note the Pineapples and Bananas growing on the slope behind the site.

There is no way we could do this in Australia. We would be charged with child abuse, and non-compliance with Work and Safety regulations. We are proud of our students who worked to pay for their education, and today many of these children are still working as adults in responsible positions in mission work or their own society.

As well as the blocks we also needed timber for our buildings. Pr John came to the rescue again. He had seen an old Oil Exploration Camp upriver, and they had just abandoned it when they left. He contacted the ones in charge in Port Moresby and went to see them personally explaining our need to use some of the equipment for a small sawmill for our school. They graciously agreed to allow us to have whatever we could use. We found a saw-bench with rollers and rail lines and trolleys which we set up at our school by a small creek off the main river. I obtained a length of flat belting and was able with a little ingenious engineering to hook up the tractor PTO, (Power Take Off), to run the sawbench. John found an old ship's winch and cable as well, but where could we get good timber trees was our next problem.

Upriver a few kilometers, were thousands of acres of untouched rain forest, owned by the government. So, we approached the ADO at Kikori, Peter Maynard, and he gave us permission to take whatever we needed. So, with a group of older boys, we would motor upriver, and fell some trees by the river bank in such a way that as soon as we had trimmed the branches and had a good straight log, we could slide it into the river, tie it in with other logs to make a raft, and then we would secure the raft to the canoe and outboard motor, and head downstream to the small creek by the mill.

We had to be very clever and precise at manoeuvring the raft to get it into the small creek and up as far as possible so we could haul the logs up to the break down area with the winch, above the bench. If we missed the creek opening, the current would sweep the raft down-stream and recovery would be nigh on impossible, but we never lost a raft, praise the Lord!

We used the little chainsaw to cut the logs into two pieces with reasonably straight flat sides to slide onto the trolleys to put these flitches over the saw-bench. There was quite a bit of heavy work at the bench as it was very difficult to cut a perfectly flat side on the flitches with the chainsaw, but it worked out OK after the first bench cut, and we used this great timber for our school and dormitories without having to buy any.

As a missionary, in these isolated areas, far from towns or cities, one has to be able to do just about anything. If the tractor needed attention, guess who had to fix it? If a building needed erecting, who had to design and build it? If a medical emergency arose, who had to be a doctor, and so on?

Fitting a new clutch to the Fordson Major.

Fixing a punctured tyre on the tractor.

Constructing a new Workshop and Machinery Shed from Bush Timber, and materials from an old Oil Camp upriver, with their permission.

I must mention one of my students here. His name was Patrick. He was about sixteen years of age, and a very strong lad for his age. He could put our forty-horsepower outboard motor on his shoulder and climb down the ladder to the river truck or the canoe, with seemingly no great effort on his part. Patrick was a great help in the saw-milling operations, and he was a really wonderful great-natured boy as well. We brought him home with us to Australia on one of our furloughs, and he worked with my dad on the cane farm at Home Hill, thoroughly enjoying the time he spent there. He was a very practical lad and could turn his hand to almost anything. If it was a hot day, he would simply cut a palm frond and weave himself a great looking shady hat in minutes. He soon mastered how to use the chain saw, and care for the machinery. He is back in his own village now, witnessing for God as best he can, and helping his own people.

Patrick, (nearest), making a hat like his friend.

Our gardens were our pride and joy. We had a few different varieties of sweet potato, taro, pineapples, paw-paws, bananas, citrus, coconuts, pumpkins, corn, and we even grew a crop of rice. We also had lots of jungle foods, such as the old staple sago, and lots of leafy greens.

Every Friday afternoon was Mumu time. The students were free to prepare for the Sabbath.

For their food they liked to make Mumus. A hole was made ready in the ground and lined with lots of stones. Then a large fire was set over it and allowed to burn down to coals. Then the coals were scooped out, as well as some extra stones, and the food parcels were placed on the hot stones.

The food parcels were made of banana leaves and contained sweet potato or taro layered with greens and copiously interspersed with freshly squeezed coconut milk.

The extra stones would be scooped back on top of the parcels, and the coals also scooped back over the parcels. Sometimes they would put wet bags over the top as well, if available, or just shovel dirt on top to cover everything and seal it all in. Our family used to look forward to Sabbath morning when Riva and Anga would usually bring us a sample of their Mumu. It was delicious!

Because of the hot wet climate, it was nigh on impossible to keep food overnight without a refrigerator, but a miraculous thing happened every Sabbath. The food they prepared for Sabbath would keep right through to Sunday morning without spoiling, just like the experience the Israelites had with the Manna in the wilderness. Amazing! God truly blesses His people when they do their best to honour Him and His special day.

Chapter 14

IT HAD TO BE HIS ANGEL

We were establishing a new school at Kitomave on the mighty Kikori River. My wife and family had a home on the rise about a kilometre from the river. Because of the constant rain, we had only one road from the house to the river which had to be constantly top-dressed with coarse crushed limestone from our small rock crusher to allow the big diesel tractor and trailer to use it. We had the girls' dormitory below us, then the school, two teachers' homes, and the boys' dormitory near the river. We also had some sheds near the river, housing the rock crusher, and workstations where we made concrete blocks out of the finely-crushed limestone for the new school building.

One day, I had to take some things to the river, using the tractor and trailer. My boy Richard, who was about six years old, and the headmaster's son, who was also Richard's age, loved to ride on the trailer, and they both were with me this day, as we made our way to the river. Our tractor's brakes were not working properly, for lack of funds to buy the needed parts, and so I used to always stop the tractor and leave it in low gear, when I stopped. The tractor engine was started by pressing down on a lever underneath the steering wheel, and I didn't want the boys to be on the tractor while I was away tending to the various work teams, so after parking the tractor at the river, I told the boys in no uncertain terms, to stay on the trailer.

Well, I was talking with the group making blocks, when the tractor suddenly started and the students shouted, "Sir, Richard's driving the tractor!" Sure enough, Richard had disobeyed and was up on the tractor and had pressed the starter lever. Being in low gear, the tractor was slowly but surely heading for the river! Richard was standing behind the steering wheel, now looking very frightened indeed.

As I ran quickly to stop the tractor by pulling the fuel stop cable on the side of the engine, I shouted to Richard to stay on the tractor. Again, he disobeyed and jumped off the tractor on the far side right in front of the big rear wheel.

I managed to stop the tractor and raced around to the other side expecting to see a very squashed little body under the wheel. What a relief it was to see him sitting beside the big wheel, safe and unhurt! When we moved the tractor, there was the imprint of his pants right in the tractor tread marks. Only an angel could have moved him so quickly out of harm's way.

Naturally, we all thanked God for His care and protection of our boy, even though he had not listened and obeyed his Daddy. Surely, we have a wonderful Heavenly Father, and we are so grateful for the Guardian Angels He assigns to each one of God's children.

Chapter 15

THE KUKA KUKAS

In the southern highlands of Papua New Guinea, live a very interesting pygmy people. Whereas the coastal people are usually tall and slender, and the highland people are a little shorter and very stocky, the pygmy people of the southern highlands are very short, less than 1.5 m tall. However, of all the Papuan and New Guinean people, the Kuka Kukas, as they are known, are the fiercest and most feared. They wear a huge bunch of grass out front suspended from the waist, and have long capes beaten out of the bark of a tree to keep them warm. They are very skilled with bow and arrows and spears, and afraid of no one!

Colin Winch explaining the wonders of flight to some budding aviators.

One weekend we were visiting Lewis and Dulcie Parker and their children at Kainantu, just a little drive from Kabiufa, and Lew said he was flying the Mission plane on Sunday, to visit the

Kuka Kukas to distribute clothing and to encourage the missionaries working for these people. He invited me and Richard my son, and Darren, Lew's son to accompany him. As I love flying, I jumped at the chance to go with him and to see these people personally would be most interesting.

Flying in Papua New Guinea is precarious and very dangerous as the country is so mountainous, and rugged, and often cloud cover can seriously obscure vision. Many of the airstrips are built on the steep slopes of the mountains, or the bottoms of valleys, and are often very short as well.

Our first stop was a village at the end of a closed valley. To approach the end of the strip to do a landing, it was necessary to do a very tight low turn, to try to touch down right near the end of the strip, so we could stop before reaching the far end. Well, we landed safely but found the grass was quite long and Lew was concerned about getting enough speed up for a successful take off when it was time to leave. We soon had a large gathering of people who were so excited at seeing us. When we unloaded and distributed the clothing, they were so grateful. Richard and Darren made friends with a couple of the Kuku Kuku boys, who showed them how to use their bows and arrows.

Richard and Darren Parker getting lessons with some young Kuka Kukas.

Departure time came and the take-off was just successful, praise the Lord! As soon as we were airborne, we had to make another very tight turn to exit the valley. The missionary pilots who fly in this rugged terrain are among the best in the world. Indeed, it is a common saying among pilots that if one can fly successfully in Papua New Guinea, one can fly anywhere on the planet! Nonetheless, our mission pilots always commit themselves and their aircraft to the care of the Lord and His ministering angels before they dare leave the ground, as they surely need His special care as I was to learn at our next stop.

Ready for Take-off down the mountain.

Lew explained that we would be landing at Usarumpia next, in the heart of the Kuka Kuka country. The airstrip was rather unique in that it was very steep, and began at the top of a huge cliff, and then ran up the side of a mountain. The visit had to be made in the morning before about 11am as after that, the downdrafts at the cliff edge became quite strong, and could drop an aircraft suddenly in its approach, causing it to fly into the cliff face.

Note the Aircraft parked at the top.

Well, we touched down successfully, and Lew had to apply full power to the engine to climb the steep slope to the parking spot at the top. Wow! What an experience! Our resident missionary met us and soon there was quite a crowd gathered around the aircraft. We were amazed at their primitive clothing and the awesome weapons they were carrying.

As I had my Polaroid camera with me, I took a few pictures, and the people were amazed to see themselves, and of course everyone then wanted a picture for themselves. I explained through our missionary as interpreter, that I only had a few shots left, but if anyone would trade me a bow as a souvenir, I would take their picture. I soon had a bow and then others wanted a picture for some arrows. I couldn't hold the bow and take pictures too, so someone took the bow, and the arrows while I took the pictures.

We had a wonderful meeting with the missionary and these dear people at the meeting house, or "house lotu". We gave them some clothing too, and they were very grateful indeed, as it can become very cold in these highland areas, even though they are near the Equator.

When it came time to board the plane, I was wondering if I would have my bow and arrows. The missionary noticed my concern and assured me that they would be given to me as we left. He explained that the Kuka Kukas may be a very primitive, and savage people, but they have strict unwritten laws they strictly follow. While traveling along a path, they may find something of value obviously belonging to someone else, and may examine it, but they will put it down again and move on. They are very honest, and any stealing is dealt with immediately with execution! Wow! Where did they get such a law? Was it a carryover from God's laws written in the hearts of all men everywhere?

Sure enough, as we were about to climb aboard, someone gave me the bow, and someone else gave me the arrows that I had traded for the pictures, and we prepared for take-off. What a strange sensation as we sped down the mountainside. It felt as though we were falling, and falling ever faster, and then suddenly, we were airborne again, as we left the ground at the cliff edge, and gazed in awe at the vast chasm below us. I take my hat off to our missionary pilots who do these trips regularly to bring hope and the love of God to these dear people.

They may be just primitive savages, but they are all candidates for salvation. We look forward to meeting them again someday and living beside them in God's Kingdom and in the earth made new. What a privilege it is to be able to share the Everlasting Gospel and God's unfathomable love for all His creation, with these dear people.

Chapter 16

UNABLE TO ADMIT WE MIGHT BE WRONG

One of our boys was very sick and we had done all we could possibly do for him at the school, so we decided that I should take him in the river truck downriver to the LMS (London Missionary Society) Hospital.

It was quite a long way, but the river truck with a forty-horsepower outboard motor was very fast, and so the sick boy and I set out for the journey early in the day. (The river truck is just a rectangular aluminium barge about two metres wide, with a turned up front and about five metres long. With a forty-horsepower outboard, it can plane on the top of the water, and we sometimes allowed students to aquaplane behind it as we went to get the mail from the Head Quarter Post Office at the

Daughter Caroline aquaplaning to get mail.

Our River Truck and Canoe.

Government Station downriver about three kilometres.)

We found the LMS Hospital fairly easily, and the folks there kindly checked the lad carefully and administered some medicine intravenously and gave me some more to give him the next day. We thanked them for their kind help and set off for the journey home.

The mouth of the Kikori River is a huge delta or series of intertwining creeks and small rivers, and it is very easy to get lost in the labyrinth of waterways, but my student was sure he knew the way, and I simply had to trust him as I had never been through the delta before. I knew we had to keep fighting the current upstream, and that sooner or later we would find the main river near the Headquarters Station.

Well, we motored on and on, and the creeks kept getting smaller and I began to question the student as to whether we were in the right stream. He assured me he knew the way, and just to keep going. Another twenty minutes or so passed and now the creek was very narrow, so I questioned the student again, and again he assured me he knew the way, and to just keep going straight ahead.

After another twenty minutes or so, the creek was not only narrow but also becoming very shallow, and eventually we could not go any further as there was a fallen log across it. Right up to this time the student was assuring me that this was the right way home!

It was then I decided to take charge as Navigator. We turned the truck around and went back the way we had come for half an hour or so, and eventually we saw a man on the bank of a large creek just outside his house.

I stopped and managed to get him to understand that we wanted to go back to Kikori Station, and he gave us the right directions. It was getting late in the afternoon, fuel was low by now, and I did not want to run out of fuel in this maze of waterways, with all the mosquitoes, and crocodiles, and so on.

Fortunately, we made it safely back to the big river and were home before dark with about ten minutes of fuel left. We really thanked the Lord for His care over us, and for bringing us home safely. It also reminded me that we should not stubbornly hold on to our own opinions, unless we are absolutely sure we are correct, because as the Word of God says, "There is a way that seems right to a man, but the ends thereof are the ways of death." Proverbs 16: 25

Chapter 17

THE SAME YESTERDAY, TODAY AND TOMORROW

Kave was a very diligent indigenous missionary working in the western Papuan Gulf area. He had a lovely family of five or six children, the youngest being under one year old when this incident happened. I had one of Kave's boys, Ian, at our school at Belepa, and also at Kitomave. I knew the family from my visits to Camp Meetings in the Turama River district, and I know this story is absolutely true.

Rainfall in the Gulf averages over three hundred and sixty inches annually, and for most of the year the rivers are in flood, carrying thousands of tons of silt and debris out to sea from the mouths of the rivers. The Turama is very unique however, in that it has a very wide funnel-shaped mouth, and as the tides come in twice daily, they back up against the river water, and as the water progresses up the funnel, it has nowhere else to go but up, creating a fast-moving wave travelling upstream faster and faster, and sometimes over two metres high.

Our Mission ship the "Uraheni"(which means "Love" in the Motu language), was anchored off a village in the Turama mouth, when we heard one of these bores coming, as they make quite a noise. The ship was hanging off the anchor and facing upstream as the river water was rushing out to sea. We decided to start the engines, haul the anchor, and face the ship downstream with the propeller turning in reverse to hold the ship stationary with the bow facing the wave in case it was a big one. When we saw the wave come around a bend in the river, it was only about one metre high, but it was still a very uncanny experience, to feel the ship rise abruptly up the wave, and now the water which had been rushing out to sea was rushing the other way, with lots of foam and debris on the leading edge. These waves happen twice a day with the tides and are known as bores.

All travel on the great rivers is done in a dugout canoe. It is simply a log which has been hollowed out, shaped somewhat like a banana and open both ends to make it easy to remove the rainwater, by sloshing the canoe back and forth to send the water flying out each end till it is emptied. Now we go back to Kave's story.

He and his wife and tiny baby, and I believe he had four other children with him, were travelling in their dugout canoe returning to their home village, from a Camp Meeting late in the afternoon, when they heard a bore coming. Their canoe was full of their sleeping mats, clothing and food supplies. They were a fair way from the shore and realized that they would not make it to shore in time, so decided to face the bore, and try to ride up over it, hoping it was not a big one.

Unfortunately, it was a fairly large bore, and though they tried to keep the canoe facing the right way, the wave tipped them out with all their gear into the boiling mass of brown water racing upstream. All Papuans are good swimmers, but it is still very difficult to keep afloat in the turbulent water. Kave was able to hold on to the upturned canoe, and by now it was starting to get dark. He kept calling and calling and eventually his wife and baby, and each one of the children made it back to the canoe as they were all being swept upstream.

Eventually, the water slowed and Kave felt the river bottom. With great difficulty they managed to reach the riverbank and dragged themselves up the muddy bank quite exhausted.

Suddenly Kave's wife let out a scream. She realized that her baby was not breathing. Apparently, it had drowned as they struggled through the waters and was lying lifeless in its mother's arms. Kave took the baby and tried to resuscitate it, but there was no response.

Kave really loved the Lord, and decided to have a prayer session, to ask God to restore their baby's life. They all prayed, even the children, but nothing happened. So, they had a second round of prayer, and still nothing happened. Kave then asked his wife if she believed God could bring her baby back to life, and she did not answer. He told her that she did not believe, and that was why God did not hear their prayer as it says in James 1: 5 and 6, and 5:15. She cried out in anguish and asked God to help her believe. They all prayed again and this time the baby began to cry, and the mother hugged it closely and nursed it. They all were so happy, praising God and thanking Him for bringing back their baby's life.

But that's not the end of the story. While they were all lying there in the mud, on the river bank, one of the children felt something bumping against his legs in the shallow water. They found it was one of their bed rolls. They were able to use it to keep themselves warm and protected through the night, before continuing on their way in the morning.

We serve a wonderful God Who does not change. He is the same yesterday, today and tomorrow. He is the same God Who raised Lazarus to life, and the widow's son and others. He still honours the faith of His people, if we will trust Him explicitly.

Kave and his wife with their seven children. Ian, the eldest son was at Belepa School with us when the incident happened. The little chap on the right is the baby boy, who was dead but is now alive, because of their faith in the Lifegiver.

Chapter 18

FALSE WITNESS

It was work time in the gardens one afternoon, when Kori, a young Year Four student, came to the teachers with a disturbing story that he had seen one of our older boys and one of the older girls, lying together under a huge, fluted root, of one of the fallen trees in the new garden! This of course, was a serious accusation, and when the teachers brought it to my attention, we called the two students in and questioned them closely.

Both of these students were normally very well behaved, and good workers. They both vigourously denied that they had done anything wrong, and it seemed they were telling the truth, but someone had to be telling a lie, and we were not sure how to determine who was telling the truth. There were no other witnesses to this alleged wrongdoing so we were very puzzled and decided to call the three students together and with the teachers we had an earnest prayer session and asked God to show us what was the truth in this matter. We then sent the students back to their various activities.

It was only a short time before Kori was carried back to us by some other students, and he was crying bitterly. He had been bitten by a snake as he worked in the garden, and he was now very sorry and asking us to forgive him for bearing false witness against the older boy and girl. Well, we were able to render first aid and Kori survived, but he learned a very valuable lesson that day, and as far as we know he has never borne false witness again.

We were also very thankful to God for answering our prayers and clearing the good names of the two older students.

Our God sees everything we do and knows our very thoughts. We should guard well our thoughts and never bear false witness against others. "Whatsoever we sow, that shall we also reap." Galatians 6:7

Chapter 19

COMPASS PROBLEMS

While building our new school at Kitomave on the Kikori River, we needed lots of building materials and supplies that we couldn't produce ourselves, so we had to bring them out from Port Moresby on the Mission ship the URAHENI.

It was a fifteen or sixteen-hour voyage. Normally, after loading the ship all day we would be ready to set sail around 6pm in the evening. That would allow us time to be clear of the reefs round Moresby, and then we would set course according to the chart, (about 300 degrees west if I remember rightly,) and set off into the night. Normally in the light of dawn after sailing all night, we would be off the Vailala mouth ready to cross the bar in daylight.

On this occasion we had a very heavy load below decks and along each side of the cabin, and a couple of tons of roofing iron across the ship over the forward hold. During the night, at about 10pm we encountered a very sudden and nasty storm. We were sailing along peacefully with our big straight eight Gardiner diesel doing about 700 revs, and I had just taken over the helm for the next two-hour watch. The helmsman's task was to keep a steady course according to the big compass right in front of the helm. I had the wheelhouse window open and was thoroughly enjoying the cool fresh ocean air as it came through the window, when all of a sudden the wind picked up great speed and within minutes the sea was like a huge boiling pot of deep gullies and ridges of black water which soon came crashing over the bows and came right through into the wheelhouse forcing me to shut the window quickly and securely.

With such a heavy load on board, the ship would rise up on a wave and then plunge down into the troughs, leaving me wondering if she would rise out of the dark water. Each plunge was a frightening experience, but the good ship rose up each time to face another huge wave and trough. No one was able to sleep, and all hands were wide awake now. This went on all night and did not subside till early in the morning.

We were so thrilled to see signs of the sun beginning to appear over the horizon and waited eagerly to spot the coastline off the Vailala bar. However, the daylight arrived and all we could see was ocean for as far as the eye could see! "Where were we?" was the question on everyone's mind. We had faithfully followed the compass course through the tempestuous seas, and should be able to see the coast, but there was no land of any kind in sight anywhere on the horizon.

We knew we must be south of Papua, so we turned the ship due north, and it was two hours before we sighted the first sign of the high mountain ranges which are the backbone of the island. Another hour's sailing brought us to the Vailala mouth and we crossed the bar safely. Everyone was so glad to be in the peaceful waters of the river, but no one had any explanation of why we were so far out to sea. We checked our charts again very carefully, and still there were no explanations.

The next trip to Moresby was made in the daylight, and we sailed on the course we usually took, with no discrepancies. When John reached the harbour in Port Moresby, he visited the Harbour Master and had him come down to the ship to check the compass for us. He found no problems. The compass was working perfectly. He then asked us what sort of cargo we had on board. John described the load and mentioned the couple of tons of roofing iron across the front hold.

Aha! A light went on in the Harbour Master's head, and he explained that the steel roofing iron, which was lying below the wheelhouse and the compass, would have deflected the compass needle sufficiently to put us so far off course overnight! A compass is a simple bipolar magnetic needle suspended in the middle, usually in a fluid inside a brass case, and the North Pole of the Compass needle always points directly to the South Pole of the earth's magnetic poles. Any steel substance placed near the compass needle magnet will pull the needle to where the steel is placed.

Well, it was good to have that problem solved. We are so thankful that the deflection took us out to sea rather than into the coast, where with such a violent storm raging through the night, we would surely have been wrecked and probably all drowned. We thanked God for His protection and care and reminded ourselves often that the only sure compass we have for our lives is the Word of God, which is a solid Rock of Truth which cannot be moved, or deflected so long as we stay with God's true Word.

There are many other versions of God's Word today, and the enemy of souls is doing a fine job of deflecting the "compass needle" sometimes just a slight deflection, to lead men astray. We have found the Versions based on the Textus Receptus or the Peshitta to be the closest to God's original Word, and we have always arrived at the port of Truth using the King James Version, and the Interlinear Scriptures based on the original manuscripts. These are our chart and compass which we have always trusted implicitly.

Our two sister ships—URAHENI and DIARI 2 at anchor in a beautiful, deep, clear mountain stream off the Turama River. We were attending a Camp Meeting for the local villages. URAHENI means "LOVE" in Motu, and DIARI means "LIGHT".

Chapter 20

TRACTOR MIRACLE

One of our permanent farmhands at Kabiufa, was a very lovable and reliable worker. We had trained him to drive our big David Brown 990 tractor and one of his responsibilities was to take care of the kitchen refuse.

I had made up a special tip-bin trailer, which was parked at the back of the kitchen. When it was full or near full, it was Micah's job to hitch the tractor to the trailer and take it down to the bottom of the farm, where there were some steep valleys with bananas growing on the slopes. Micah would back the trailer to the edge of the slope and tip the bin so that it's contents would tumble out and down the slope to rot down and provide organic fertilizer for the bananas.

We never could figure out what happened on one occasion, but somehow Micah lost control of the tractor, and it began rolling down the slope over and over all the way to the bottom with Micah still on board as it rolled! We all expected he would have been crushed to death, but when we rushed down to the spot where the tractor came to rest, the right way up, we found Micah lying under the tractor unconscious, with the cushion from the tractor seat under his head. Unbelievable, but true!

We hurriedly checked his vital signs, and his pulse and breathing was normal. He seemed quite unharmed and apparently was simply winded, because he soon came to, and sat up! Micah was as amazed as we were and could only praise God for His care and the protection of His angels.

At the same time there was a contractor nearby who operated a huge forest logging machine. He graciously offered to come and retrieve our tractor from the bottom of the valley. With a powerful winch attached and myself astride the steering wheel he was able to drag our tractor back to the top of the slope, and back on to level ground.

We soon had the tractor repaired as it was not badly damaged. This was another amazing thing, and we thanked our Heavenly Father again for His care not only of Micah, but also of our machinery. What an amazing God we serve!

Chapter 21

I DIDN'T LISTEN

Because many of our Kabiufa students came from the coastal areas of Papua New Guinea, and were used to having coconuts in their diet, I would periodically make the long trip to Lae with my Holden Wagon and trailer to buy coconuts for the student menu. Ruth was in charge of the Kabiufa Dining Room for some time and the students learned to eat fresh salads as well as the staple cooked sweet potato and corn. Coconut milk made the food very tasty indeed, and more nutritious. Their grades increased remarkably with the fresh food included in their daily fare.

On one of my trips I had Patrick, one of my senior students with me. We stopped at Kainantu, and checked fuel, tyres, and the connection with the trailer. All seemed in order so we set off for Lae and soon began negotiating the rugged Kassam Pass.

This is the road leading down from the Highlands to the Markham Valley and Lae.

The road down the Pass was only gravel and very rough.
Only some of the road had bitumen as we came closer to Lae.

We had almost reached "the bottom of that terrible descent" winding back and forth down the mountainside, when we came to a kilometer or so of straight section with bitumen. As soon as I saw the straight road I was so relieved, but I distinctly had an impression to stop and check the trailer. It was as though a little voice was urging me to stop and check the trailer hitch. Should I stop now? The straight bitumen road ahead looked so inviting. I argued with myself and assured myself that we had checked the trailer hitch at the top and it was OK, so I took my foot off the brakes and let the car roll faster and faster down this lovely smooth road.

Suddenly Patrick shouted, "Sir, the trailer has come off!" Sure enough, I looked up into the rear vision mirror, and there was the trailer coming down the road behind us but not joined to our car as it should be! It was somersaulting down the road end for end, and came to rest, right side up, right beside the road! Whew! What a shock! If only I had listened to that still small voice.

Well, on closer inspection, the damage was mostly to the front of the trailer. Apparently the ball had worked loose on the rough road and had become disconnected from the towbar. It could easily have tumbled over the edge and landed far down the mountainside. How blessed we were that it ended up right there beside the road.

The cup on the trailer hitch was wrecked, but we found some old fencing wire nearby, and were able to make a temporary connection to the car which enabled us to drive the rest of the way to Lae. We found a workshop where we were able to do the necessary, and costly repairs, and after considerable delay, were able to continue with our goal of finding a load of coconuts to take home to Kabiufa.

We were so thankful that the damage was not a lot worse. That lesson has stayed with me for many years, and now I always try to respond to that still small voice. I believe it was the Holy Spirit speaking to me, and if only I had listened, I would not have had to pay a nasty repair bill and would have saved myself considerable delay as well.

Chapter 22

MT WILHELM

One of my responsibilities whilst at Kabiufa, was to oversee the Gold and Silver Medallion courses for the College students. As part of that self-sufficiency training they had to do a three day wilderness trek and camp out. Each year I would take a group of seven or eight of these older students and travel to Kegsugl Village, which is quite high, near the base of Mt Wilhelm. Wilhelm is the highest mountain in the country. It is over 15,000 feet above sea level. Snow and ice can be found at the top all year round, and reaching the top is quite an achievement.

To reach Kegsugl we would travel by vehicle for about three hours, then we would hire a couple of porters for the teacher's gear, and climb up the first grassy valley to our first overnight

stop at the Lakes at an elevation of about 11,000 feet.

Crossing one of the many bush bridges on the way. A frightening experience in itself.

These three lakes were set one above the other with the water from the top one overflowing to the second and then the largest one at the campsite. Some of our coastal students saw the beautiful blue water and asked if they could go for a swim. It was very amusing to see how quickly they got out of that freezing water off the melting summit ice.

Crossing one of the many bush bridges on the way. A frightening experience in itself.

Looking down on the first lake from the second.

Quick exit from the freezing water.

There were a few small grass huts by the lakes, which we slept in.

Ralph Murray, Pr Lui Oli's son, and Ross Bellinger shaving.

Early the next morning, we would leave to ascend the first ridge on our way to the summit. Just below the ridge is the wreckage of an allied bomber which slammed into the ridge during the war. It was about fifty feet below what was needed to clear the ridge. So near and yet so far. At the top of that first ridge, we could see another deep wide valley and it is the only place where I have heard a full sentence echo. We would call out, "How are you?" and the echo would come back in full. We called again, "What is your name?" and the echo returned, "What is your name?" On one trek, we reached the top of the ridge just on sunrise and were rewarded with a view of the coast to the north. Because it was a perfectly clear day with no clouds at all, we could even pick out the ships and boats at anchor at Madang Harbour.

The view from the top of the first ridge above the lakes.

On one of our trips, one of the student girls was very sick with some stomach ailment, when we reached the lakes. She was still sick in the morning, so I volunteered to stay with her, while the rest of the party made assault on the summit, which was a full day's trek including the return to the Lakes Camp. To pass the time, I decided to cook some rice for dinner, so I gathered some small sticks and grass, as there are no trees growing at that altitude, just small hardy shrubs here and there.

Soon I had the fire going well and the billy was boiling in a very short time, so in went the rice. I had brought whole-grain rice and after ten or fifteen minutes I tried the rice to see if it was softening. It was still as hard as when it went in! So, I stoked the fire and waited for half an hour and tested the rice again. It was still as hard as when it went in!! So, I made the fire "seven times hotter" and gave it another half hour, but with the same result. I realized something was wrong when, despite the water boiling vigorously, I could comfortably hold my finger in it. At 11,000 feet above sea level, the air pressure is much less dense than at sea level, and therefore the boiling point of water is much lower. I never did get to eat that rice but learned a valuable lesson in Science.

Looking up from the bottom lake to the overflow from above.

Usually, we would reach the summit about mid-morning, and it was quite a thrill to stand on top of the highest mountain in the country, with snow and ice around us. What a view we would have on a clear day from that "eagle's perch"! Wilhelm is twice as high as Kosciusko. Papua New Guinea is a very mountainous country compared to Australia. It is said that pilots who fly in Papua New Guinea are among the best in the world.

Pockets of unmelted snow and ice near the summit.

On one occasion, I had two of my children with me in the group, Jennelle and Richard. When we reached the top of the first ridge, the sun was really hot, and we were all sweating profusely. Rather than carry our heavy warm clothing with us we decided to leave the warm stuff under some rocks and proceed to the summit without them. Well, that was not a good decision. We had only been climbing for about an hour when the weather changed very suddenly, the wind began blowing hard, and clouds rolled in over us. Soon it was sleeting and my beard soon had icicles hanging from it. Just nearby, fastened to a huge rock, was a Warning Sign.

It was in memory of an army chap who was lost in a similar blizzard and was never found. Presumably, he took a wrong path, not able to see the path markers, and must have fallen over a precipice. Richard was very cold, so I took off my second pair of long socks and put them on his legs and kept going. He looked quite a sight with my long socks right up his little legs. We made it to the top and were so glad the blizzard eased off as we made our way down again. We were all very thankful to our Heavenly Father for His care.

Yes, that's where we're going! The summit. Over 15,000feet.

Success! The highest point in Papua New Guinea. Over twice as high as Kosciusko.

Many of these wonderful young people finished their training and are now occupying very responsible positions in their villages, schools, hospitals and even in Government, upholding the way of life they have been taught in our schools and colleges. My wife and I will always be grateful for the opportunity to be a part of their training. Some of them still keep contact with us today.

Chapter 23

THE HIGHLANDS

After serving for seven years in the hot, wet, steamy jungles of the Papuan Gulf, our transfer to Kabiufa College in the Highlands, near Goroka, was like moving to heaven. The climate was so different because of the elevation. Nearness to the Equator meant that the day length remained almost the same all year round, and we needed blankets to sleep comfortably each night. It was so refreshing to rise each morning after a beautiful sleep, to work in a temperature and air density so different to the oppressive, hot, heavy air of the Papuan Gulf.

Beautiful Poinsettia in the Campus gardens.

Our school at Kabiufa was a really delightful place, situated in the Goroka Valley. It had a barret or small creek running right through the one hundred and seventy odd acres of fertile valley soil. The climate was ideal for growing all sorts of vegetables, and fruits, although the trees that needed seasons did not know when to flower and fruit. We had two huge Avocado trees in our yard, and there was only a very short period when they were not fruiting. We enjoyed Avocadoes or Butter Fruit as the local people called them, pretty well all year round.

One morning as we were sitting down to breakfast, there was a large cracking sound followed by a heavy thud. We found that a large branch had broken off the Avocado tree. The branch was so laden with fruit that it could not support the weight and broke away from the tree. These Avocadoes were the size of baseballs, and we gathered a whole builder's wheelbarrow full to take to the College Store. They were truly delicious fruit too.

Not long after we arrived, we met the local chieftain, whose name, given to him by the College Staff, was "Greasy"! He didn't know much English, but there were two words he had mastered—"Gimme"! He would point to different articles and say "Gimme" and was very put out if one did not give him what he wanted.

One morning he appeared at our front door, with two pineapples he offered to sell me. They were good pineapples, so I gave him some money for them to keep him happy, as we had our own pineapple patch in the back garden and didn't really need to buy his.

When I went inside and showed the family, the children said, "Dad, they look the same as ours!" and then the "penny clicked". Sure enough, when we checked the back garden, the fruit we were watching to pick were missing. Greasy had picked our pineapples and sold them to us at the front door! Hmmm! He was not popular at our home after that, and we realized that his name was indeed appropriate.

Kabiufa College and High School, catered for about one hundred and fifty students, with a large staff of ex-patriot and indigenous teachers and some local people as labourers. The school system was built on the same model as our primary schools, with a Work/Study plan. At Kabiufa, half the student body would be out working in the gardens, the farm, maintenance, and kitchen, while the other half were at classes. Then at changeover times, they would swap positions. This plan ensured that there were workers available all day for the gardens and industries, and of course classes could also continuc all day.

Student body on Parade.

Staff members of Kabiufa High School and College.

Kabiufa Market Gardens had their own full-time manager, and Sales Manager, and a Store situated by the highway that ran through the property. Each day plane loads of produce would be shipped out of Goroka to all parts of Papua New Guinea. Our Market Gardens were the largest market Gardens in the Southern Hemisphere at the time. The income from the Gardens provided support for many activities and workers right throughout the Mission field.

Some of the Market Gardens with students working.

Carrots and Beans growing in the rich valley soil.

Thousands of seedlings ready for transplanting.

Some of the Garden Produce for sale at the Roadside Store.

The Market Garden Store.

About the year 1970, the Papua New Guinea Government brought in their National Education Scheme, and invited all the various Missions to join their scheme, and they would then grant funds to the Missions to pay their teachers and other expenses. We considered their proposal but decided that we would stay separate and keep a clear distinction between our system of education and the Government's.

If we joined the national Scheme, they would provide funding, but we would have to abide by their educational guidelines. We would have to accept their teachers on our staff, and we would have to follow their Curriculum as well.

A delegation of Government Education people arrived one day, and as I happened to be just finishing a class, I was invited by the Principal to meet them and listen to what they had to say. They were concerned that we would not join their National Education Scheme, and one chap asked the question, "If you are not getting our funding, how long do you think you will be able to operate?"

Well, that opened the door for the Principal to explain our system of Work/Study, and how our industries, not only provided the funding for our operations but they also provided funds for a great deal of the rest of the Mission needs as well. It also provided the students a means to pay their school fees. They were "blown away" by our system, and said, "We wish we had such a great system!" Following God's plan is always the best plan. Sometime later, I was speaking with leaders of the other Missions, and they were lamenting that they had joined the Government scheme, and were wishing that they had stayed separate, as we had done. They had teachers appointed to their schools who did not love the Lord and had to allow heathen tribal dances and cultures to be practised in their schools. We were so glad we had stayed with the Lord's directives, and He blessed our schools abundantly.

Some of our Student Youth at Kabiufa.

School Captains.

My Kabiufa Gym Club on display.

Springboard and Box Work.

Forward Somersault off Spring Board.

Relaxing by the barret during Recess.

Graduating Class of about 1972.

Mrs Brown and the Girls' Choir.

The Old Chapel with thatched roof and bush timber construction.

Graduates ready for service in their Lord's Vineyard.

As well as my teaching load in the High School and College, it was my responsibility, to feed the students and staff, as the Farm Manager. I had about one hundred acres of lovely valley soil, two tractors and machinery, and of course plenty of student labour with a couple of indigenous work supervisors full time. Teachers also were rostered to work with the students as supervisors as well. We grew Sweet Potatoes and Corn as our main crops, and also had Peanuts, Soybeans, Bananas, and various other food crops as well.

Two of our girls preparing sweet potato in the barret, for the kitchen.

Students threshing soybeans from the farm.

The Dining Room ready for Lunch.

My farming experience stemmed from my boyhood, as I was brought up on a farm in North Queensland. I had become absolutely convinced that Sustainable Agriculture was only achievable by employing Organic Farming methods, and I followed these principles as closely as possible using Green Manuring, Crop Rotation, and Composting. Our crops were quite remarkable with high yields and good quality produce to feed our hungry students and staff.

(As often happens, the Mission administration began urging the Garden Manager to try to increase the garden profits, to provide more and more funds for the ever-expanding needs of the Mission. Unfortunately, artificial fertilizer usage was stepped up to provide higher yields, and after some time, some garden areas were so depleted that they would not even grow a cabbage. After three years managing the College Farm, the Administration decided I would be transferred to be in charge of Maintenance, and the Garden Manager would take over management of the farm as well, allowing him to use the farm area for the Market Garden, thus bringing in more and more money, with little thought to the consequences and sustainability. What it is like now I do not know.)

Papua New Guinea is prone to earthquake activity, and on numerous occasions while at Kabiufa, we had earth tremors with the water in the tanks sloshing from side to side, and the lights swinging from side to side. One tremor felt as though a bulldozer had just hit the house, but we never had any serious damage happen while we were there.

On one occasion, while at Mission Headquarters at Lae, we were sitting in the upstairs room. During the meeting, I looked out the window and could not believe my eyes! About three or four blocks away the houses were rising and then they descended, and the next lot of houses rose and descended and the next until we were rising, quite gently as if on a wave! What an uncanny experience and one I shall never forget.

Not too far from Kabiufa there were some underground caves, which were largely unexplored. Some staff and some students banded together to do an exploration trip in these caves. My daughter Wendy and a friend she knew from Goroka were with us. We had wet weather gear and of course, torches and spare batteries.

We descended into the first cave and climbed down a long way following a passageway with a stream at the bottom. The stalactites and stalagmites were wondrous formations to behold. As we followed further and further along the passage, the ceiling was noticeably becoming lower and lower, and the wind roaring past us was quite strong. Eventually we could not stand up and had to bend over till we came to a place where the ceiling was only about a foot from the floor with the wind howling through. We were expecting to see an opening, but all was pitch black. When we switched the torches off it was a very chilling eerie experience.

Some of us decided we wanted to see what was further on so we literally wriggled on our stomachs through this narrow space, which opened up on the other side to a large cavern. Between the floor of the narrow space, and the ceiling the stalactites and stalagmites had made a forest of pillars, some being six inches or more thick, and we had to negotiate through this calcite jungle to reach the other side about twenty feet through in all.

Wendy came through after me, and there was only her friend left on the other side. Suddenly she let out a scream and began crying and saying she couldn't do it, so Wendy went back to her and helped her through. The effort was really worth it as this new cave had obviously never been visited before it seemed. The formations were so fine and exquisitely beautiful. We took some lovely pictures and were so glad to have seen these wonderful works of nature unspoiled by human hand.

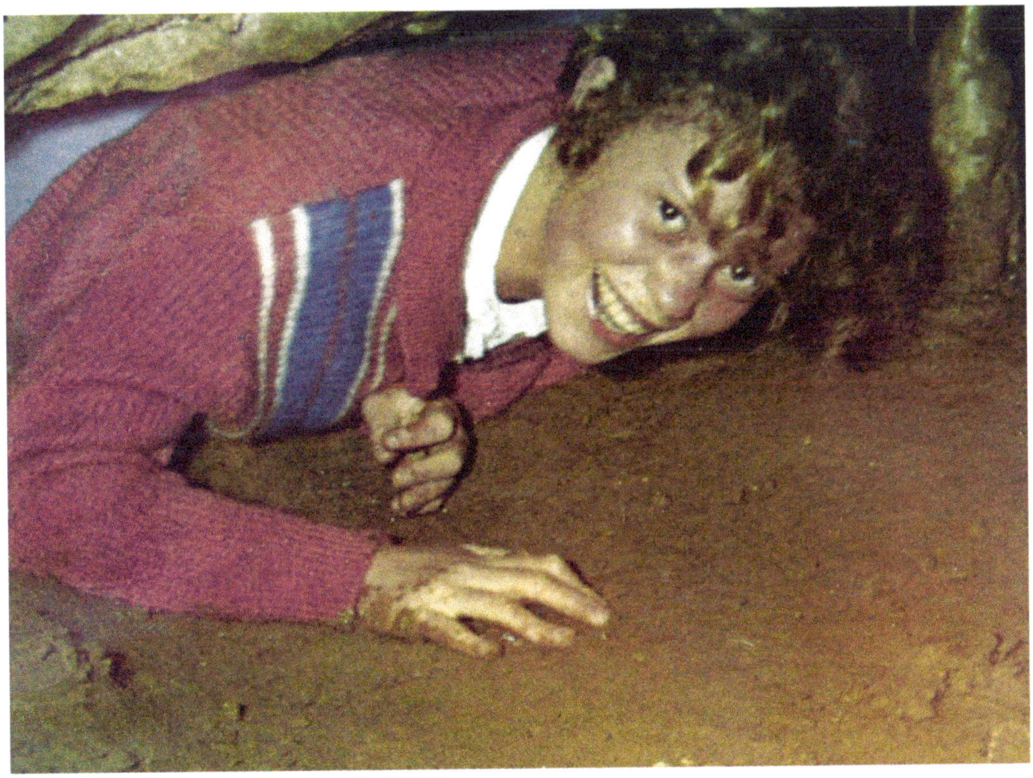

Daughter Wendy wriggling through the opening.

Exquisite Limestone Formations possibly seen for the first time.

When my Dad was visiting us once we took a trip to Sopas to see our hospital there near Mt Hagen. We stopped at one spot to admire the views, and my Dad took out his mouth organ and began playing some tunes. Very soon a crowd of local people gathered, intrigued by these new sounds. One of the older chaps, with a big red mouth from eating betelnut wanted right or wrong to play Dad's mouth organ.

Dad didn't like the idea and for some reason he stopped playing and took his teeth out. The effect on the crowd was incredible. They all disappeared instantly, and we had no further trouble.

Our four years at Kabiufa were generally very happy ones, but as our children were growing older, we wanted to have them complete their education in Australia, and so at the end of 1973, we left PNG on permanent return to work for the Lord at home in Australia.

Chapter 24

ONGOING MISSION

My commitment to serving my fellow men as a missionary teacher, did not end when we came home to Australia. For six years we served at Mullumbimby and inspired the community there to build a lovely new school on Main Arm Road.

Then we took an appointment at Macquarie Fields in Sydney thinking that our children would have opportunity to complete their education in the Adventist High School at Strathfield. In hindsight, it was a wrong move as our children could not cope with city life, and influences, after having lived in only country areas for so long.

After four years at Macquarie Fields, we were asked to take charge of the school at Townsville. I had been teaching continuously for thirty years and at the end of 1984 we retired to have a change and do further studies in the fields of Natural Health and Healing. We used our training and experience in Natural Healing—God's Way--to run four fourteen-week courses at Kingaroy at the TAFE College, and then we accepted a call from Jonathan Gray, to do a Training Course in New Zealand.

This was a real challenge, but I love challenges. Jonathan had four lovely young people ready to come—Vijay from India, Juhyun from Korea and two girls, Satoe and Ai, from Okinawa.

Our three girls in National Costumes of Japan and Korea.

I taught the Japanese girls English for some time before the course began. They were very intelligent and gifted young people and soon had a grasp of the English language sufficient to begin the training course, which lasted for six months in very concentrated form, with lectures all morning, and practical exercises in the afternoons.

We had found a beautiful property for a Health Retreat at Ruamahunga Bay just north of Thames, and had guests who needed help and treatments, which were administered by the students under our supervision. Mark Tyree was a Colporteur in the area, and he was able to find people in the community who needed help with their health, so our students ventured out to their homes to give treatments and advice to the needy ones. Many wonderful experiences occurred, and many sick people were helped physically and spiritually as well.

By the end of the course, each student was able to give a lecture to community groups, explaining the principles for Health and Happiness by following God's Eight Natural Laws of Health—Proper Nutrition,

Food Art by Juhyun I Believe.

Preparing a Nutritious Meal.

Adequate Exercise, the importance of Water, using Sunshine wisely, the importance of Temperance, (avoiding the bad things, and using the good in moderation,) getting good Fresh Air, adequate Rest, and Trust in Our Creator.

Class Time—A&P Theory

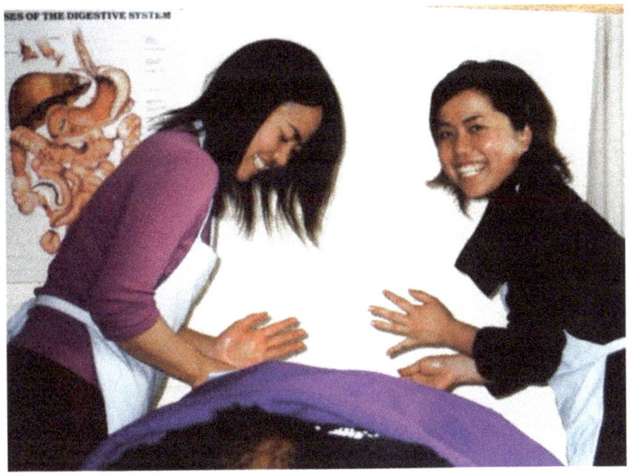

Practical—Ai and Satoe giving Vijay the "works".

Vijay lecturing a group of older people.

One older man came to the Retreat, with serious heart troubles, and a frozen knee joint. He had about a dozen different pills for all his problems, and we started working with him, with massage, steam baths, cleansing baths and specific supplements and treatments to detox his system.

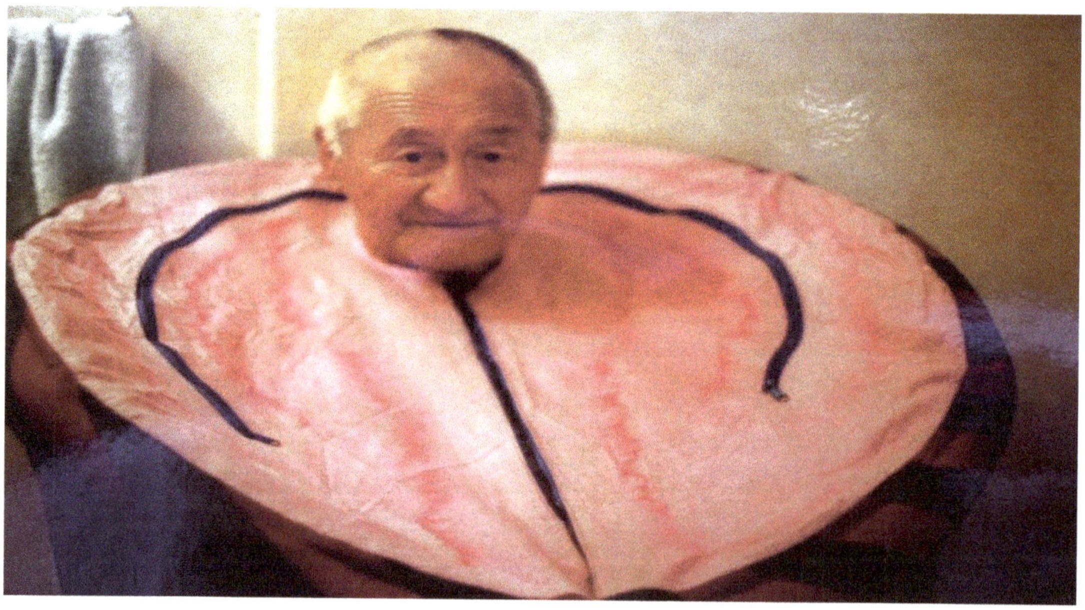

An older guest enjoying his daily Steam Bath.

One day as we were massaging his frozen knee with Castor Oil, there was a very audible cracking noise, and he discovered he could now move his knee joint. Amazing! Unbeknown to us, he had not been taking his pills for the ten days, with no repercussions fortunately. He walked out of the Retreat feeling very much better and very happy.

On another occasion our girls went to the home of a man in Thames suffering with Arthritis, which made it very difficult for him to walk. They suggested he start drinking six to eight glasses of good water each day, and just making that change and following their advice, when they next visited, he was riding his bicycle! The students were thrilled to see the effects of following God's Plan for Health and Healing, and we had numerous other wonderful experiences as well.

At the end of the course, we had a Graduation in Thames and invited many guests and Gary Martin from Living Valley Springs Retreat in Australia as Guest Speaker. It was a very wonderful day, and so fulfilling to see these fine young people equipped to share God's ways of Health and Healing in their various areas of the world. The girls were extremely talented musicians, and thrilled everyone present with their music.

The musical trio. All had great voices, but Satoe was incredible at Piano also. Juhyun was very able on the Flute, and Ai could sing like a Lark!

We really treasure the memories of working with these talented young people who are still using their training to help those in need.

For me it has been a very soul-satisfying experience to use the talents the Lord provided for me, in spreading His Gospel through teaching and practical healing work instead of chasing the allurements that the world has to offer.

Graduates with two of their Teachers.

The Graduates and Guest Speaker Gary Martin.

Ruth and I were still teaching and sharing God's ways of healing, when the Lord put my precious companion to rest, very peacefully but unexpectedly, in 2016. After sixty-four years of working together as teachers, missionaries and Natural Health practitioners and instructors at Home in Australia and abroad in Papua and New Guinea for eleven years, and also in New Zealand, I was suddenly all alone without my precious companion.

After Ruth died, my Lord found me another lovely lady, Naomi, with virtually the same goals and lifestyle as myself, and we plan to continue sharing God's Plan of Salvation and Natural Healing, as long as we still have Health and Strength to do so. As I complete writing this book, it is 2026.

God's way of healing, whether the problem be physical, mental or spiritual, is to find the cause and eradicate habits, practices and toxic overloads that cause disease and suffering, for as the Scriptures state very plainly, **"The curse, <u>causeless</u>, shall not come."** Proverbs 26:2

"Without health the richest man is poor!"

Chapter 25

WHILE THE DOOR IS STILL OPEN

Again, I would like to give thanks to my beautiful wife, Ruth, and to our five wonderful children, for their participation with us through many very rough and trying times that we experienced in the Papuan Gulf for seven years.

At Goroka Airport

Moving to the Highlands at Kabiufa High School and College near Goroka, was such a dramatic change from the very hot, wet, steamy jungles of the Gulf. We spent four years at Kabiufa and enjoyed the lovely Highland Climate and Work there.

Listening to Kata Ragoso's story that I have already shared with you in this book, is what motivated me to dedicate my life as a Missionary; to sharing the Gospel with the dear people of the Pacific Islands when I was just nine or ten years old. It has been so rewarding to see so many of our young people and older people from the surrounding areas, committing their lives to the Lord and preparing to share the blessed hope of eternal life in a completely renewed earth, with our Saviour for eternity! No more pain, sickness, crime or death forever! All doctors, nurses, health workers and funeral directors will be "out of a job"! John Newton's lovely old hymn, "Amazing Grace" says:

"When we've been there ten thousand years,

Bright shining as the sun,

We've no less days to sing God's praise,

Than when we first begun!"

It is now as I write this, it is 2026 AD, almost six thousand years since our first parents decided to disobey our Lord's specify command and believe in the lie of the Serpent, Satan. In the Word of God, the Bible, and the prophecies there in **Daniel and Revelation, and the Gospels; Matthew 24, Mark 11, and Luke 21,** we find the signs that the end of this sin, suffering and death, is about to end. For proof of this, go to my website and download the **FREE** Booklets **"It's All About Love"**, and **"True Australian Story"**.

The two major signs, that show we are indeed very close to the end, are found in Daniel Chapter 12 verses 1-4. **"Knowledge shall be increased, and men shall run to and fro."**

The explosion of knowledge in every facet of life, with men running to and fro, **just in my lifetime of only 90 years has been astronomical!**

The opportunity to avail ourselves of the "blessed hope" <u>is still available</u>, before the Lord says, **"Enough, close the door!"**

Just as in the time of Noah, after 120 years of Noah's preaching, the door of the Ark was finally closed, and only those who accepted the offer of salvation were saved from the worldwide flood. The Saviour is still knocking at the door of our hearts. There is no handle on the outside of our heart's door. **It must be opened from the inside**! You and I have to use our God-given **FREEWILL** and **choose** to Open the Door and let Jesus in, or leave it closed, as so many are doing today.

In Matthew 24: 36-39, Jesus said,

"But of that day and hour no man knows, not even the angels of heaven, but my Father only. But as it was in the days of Noah, so shall also the coming of the Son of Man be. For as in the days that were before the flood, people were eating and drinking, marrying and giving in marriage, until the day that Noah entered the Ark. They did not listen to the warnings, till the flood came and took them all away!" (My Modern Translation.)

Amazing evidence of the worldwide flood is documented in my other published books, also available at my website.... **getwellnstaywell.com**

Here are some lovely Scriptures, showing God's unfathomable love for His Creation:

John 14:1-3 **"Let not your heart be troubled: you believe in God, believe also in Me.**

In my Father's house are many mansions: if it were not so, I would have told you. I go to prepare a place for you.

And if I go and prepare a place for you, I will come again and receive you unto Myself; that where I am, there you may be also."

Psalms 36:7 **"How priceless is your unfailing love, O God! People take refuge in the shadow of your wings."**

Romans 5:8 **"But God demonstrates His own love for us in this: while we were still sinners, Christ died for us."**

1 John 4:10-12 "**Herein is love, not that we loved God, but that He loved us, and sent His Son to be the propitiation for our sins.**

Beloved, if God so loved us, we ought also to love one another.

No man has seen God at any time. If we love one another, God dwells in us, and His love is perfected in us."

Ephesians 3:19 **"And to know the love of Christ, which passes knowledge, that you might be filled with all the fullness of God."**

Jeremiah 29:11 **"For I know the thoughts I think toward you, saith the Lord, thoughts of peace, and not of evil, to give you an expected end."**

John 3:16 and 17 **"For God so loved the world, that He gave His only begotten Son, that whosever believeth in Him should not perish, but have everlasting life.**

For God sent not His Son into the world to condemn the world, but that the world through Him might be saved."

1 Thessalonians 4: 13-18 and 1 Corinthians 15: 51-57 are also wonderful Scriptures showing how this 6000-year-old demonstration of God's Kingdom, the **Kingdom of LOVE**, compared with Satan's **Kingdom of Force,** will end!

I would like to invite everyone who reads this little book, to consider accepting the wonderful gift of salvation; to exercise your God-given **FREEWILL** and **choose** to "**open the door**" to let Jesus into your heart and life. The wages of sin is death but the war between Good and Evil has been won and the penalty has been paid in full at Calvary.

All Praise to our Wonderful Heavenly Father, to our Blessed Saviour Jesus Christ, and the Holy Spirit Who leads us into all Truth.

Please consider joining with me as a **Missionary,** to share the **Gospel**, the **Good News**, and the **Good Health message**, and the **Eight Laws of Health**, with wherever and with whosoever we meet, **while the door of God's Kingdom is still open**!

With love to all, and malice toward none,

Don Menkens.

ABOUT THE AUTHOR

Don Menkens was born in Townsville in 1935. He grew up in North Queensland. After graduating from High School, he worked on his grandfather's cane farm for a year to earn enough money to go to Avondale College at Cooranbong, in New South Wales, to train as a builder. From the age of ten he planned to work as a Missionary in the Islands of the Pacific to build schools and churches for the island people, where they could learn about God and His love.

Because he was only seventeen his work-study programme at Avondale soon devoured all his savings. He saw that he could not complete the Building Course, so for a while he tried Colporturing in Brisbane, but that was not successful either, because of the rainy season. Books and rain don't mix well. So, on the advice of some friends, he enrolled at the Queensland Teachers College and completed the Teaching Course.

After working for the Queensland Education Department for a while, he was called by the Seventh Day Adventist Church to be Principal of the aboriginal school at Mona Mona, near Cairns, where he taught for two years, before being asked to take charge of a large school at Belepa in the Papuan Gulf as Principal with seven staff.

He also pioneered a new school further round the Gulf on the Kikori River. Three hundred acres of tropical jungle and a budget of $300 was quite a challenge, but the school was established and is still operating today, 2026. He and his wife Ruth spent seven years in the hot, wet, steamy jungles of the Papuan Gulf before being transferred to Kabiufa High School and College near Goroka in the New Guinea Highlands for four years. What a very welcome change of climate that was!

With his wife Ruth and their five children they returned to Australia in 1973, so their older children could continue higher education in Australia. He was Principal of a new school he planned and organized at Mullumbimby for six years, before taking charge of Macquarie Fields school in Sydney for four years. He then was posted to Townsville and retired after a year there in 1984.

They bought a small acreage of land near Kingaroy and developed a small farm and Earthworm Business for ten years. They also trained as Natural Health teachers and taught Swedish Massage at Kingaroy TAFE College for three years. They also helped set up Health Centres at Kangaroo Valley, in NSW, New Zealand on the Coromandel Peninsula, Living Valley near Kin Kin in Qld and elsewhere.

He lost his dear **Ruth** in 2016, after sixty-four years together, just before her eighty-first birthday. The Lord put her to sleep very peacefully but unexpectedly. How he found and married a lovely widow from the Blue Mountains, in 2017, is told in his book titled **"IT'S ALL ABOUT LOVE"** and is quite a story! You can find his other books and FREE Booklets, at his website: getwellnstaywell.com

His new companion is **Naomi**. **Ruth** and **Naomi** is a real romance drama, old style, in the Old Testament in the Book of Ruth. For eight years, they have enjoyed retirement at Landsborough on the Sunshine Coast of Queensland.

Presently, **2026**, Naomi is in Garden Village, in Port Macquarie, near her eldest daughter, receiving care for a skin condition she has been suffering from for some years. Don is still living in their home at Landsborough, and is able to visit his Naomi from time to time.

Don is still doing Missionary work, writing and publishing Books and FREE Booklets, for anyone interested in how the Word of God portrays the future. The Lord's promise of eternal life in a re-created "Garden of Eden Earth" is very appealing to Don!

What a blessed hope instead of a hopeless end!

Don invites you to **choose** to join with him,

"WHILE THE DOOR IS STILL WIDE OPEN".

www.ingramcontent.com/pod-product-compliance
Ingram Content Group UK Ltd.
Pitfield, Milton Keynes, MK11 3LW, UK
UKHW061959290726
14090UKWH00021B/1290

9 781764 477222